Kennikat Press
National University Publications
Series in Political Science

POLITIC

POLITICS,
PROGRAMS,
and BUREAUCRATS

WILLIAM P. BROWNE

National University Publications
KENNIKAT PRESS // 1980
Port Washington, N.Y. // London

Manufactured in the United States of America

Published by
Kennikat Press Corp.
Port Washington, N.Y. / London

Library of Congress Cataloging in Publication Data

Browne, William Paul, 1945-
    Politics, programs, and bureaucrats.

    (Political science series) (National university
publications)
    Includes bibliographical references and index.
    1. Administrative agencies—United States.
2. United States—Politics and government. 3. Bureaucracy. I. Title. II. Series: Political science
series (Port Washington, N.Y.)
JK421.B76   353'.01   79-27407
ISBN 0-8046-9263-7

CONTENTS

SECTION ONE: BUREAUCRACY

1. BUREAUCRACY, BUREAUS, AND PROGRAMS   **3**

      The Cloak of Bureaucratic Invisibility / 7

      Politics and Administration as One / 9

      What Is "Bureaucracy"? / 11

      Bureau Activity / 15

      Bureaus Never Work Alone / 19

      Bureaucrats / 23

2.   **THE BUREAU OF MINES AT WORK**   **27**

      Its Mission / 30

      Research / 31

      Implementation and Regulation / 33

      Success and Failure / 36

      Its Value to Others / 38

SECTION TWO: THE POLITICAL ENVIRONMENT OF BUREAUCRACY

3. POLITICAL INSTITUTIONS AND THE BUREAU   **45**

      Executive Leadership / 48

      Legislative Politics / 50

      Interest Groups / 55

      Whirlpools of Activity / 57

      A Case Study of Political Influence / 60

4. BUREAUS AND THE BUREAUCRACY   **65**

      Control Agencies / 65

      Bureaucratic Hierarchy / 69

      Horizontal Cooperation / 74

      Regionalism / 76

      Intergovernmental Relations / 78

      A Case Study of Bureaucratic Conflict / 81

SECTION THREE: THE WORK OF BUREAUCRACY

5. DEVELOPING PROGRAMS IN A MAZE   89
Political Concerns / 90
Bureau Organization / 92
Fact Finding / 94
Interpretation / 96
Recommendation and Advocacy / 98

6. OPERATING GOVERNMENT PROGRAMS   103
More Planning / 104
The Focus of Implementation / 107
Coordination and Implementation / 111
Evaluating Programs / 114

7. BUREAUCRACY'S IRON GLOVE: Regulation   120
Formal Power / 122
Rule-making / 125
Regulation, Justice, and the Courts / 127
The Problem of Coordination / 131
Political Responses to Regulation / 133

SECTION FOUR: POLITICAL CHANGE AND THE BUREAUCRACY

8. BUREAUCRACY THREATENED—THE POLITICS OF THE 1970's   143
The 1976 Election / 143
Carter's Reorganization / 146
Setting New Agendas / 153

9. FUTURE PROSPECTS :
A Conclusion about Public Bureaucracy   159
Political Responsibility / 161
Public Service / 163
The Participant's Dilemma / 164
And Finally, the Future Will Be the Present / 166

NOTES   171

INDEX   177

POLITICS, PROGRAMS, and BUREAUCRATS

ABOUT THE AUTHOR

William P. Browne is Professor of Political Science at Central Michigan University. He has been involved educationally with a variety of federal agencies including the Department of Defense and the Law Enforcement Assistance Administration. His writings have appeared in numerous journals and he has presented papers at meetings of many of the national and regional associations of political scientists and public administrators in the United States. He is the author of *The New Politics of Food* (1978) and *The Role of U.S. Agriculture in Foreign Policy* (1979).

SECTION ONE

BUREAUCRACY

1 . . .

BUREAUCRACY, BUREAUS, and PROGRAMS

American government is composed of a complex maze of interrelated political institutions. There is the President, who, at the national level, directs by executive orders, executive agreements, and his position as head of government. (See Table 1.1.) He shares power with a Congress which passes laws in the form of legislative acts. Then too there is the Judiciary with its power to hand down court decisions on the constitutionality of government rules and regulations. The existence of parallel sets of institutions at the state and local levels further complicates this framework of separated powers and checks and balances. (See Tables 1.2 and 1.3.)

Despite this perplexing array of government bodies, an American citizen who is unfamiliar with any one of them is a rarity. Most people are aware of the work performed by these decision-makers just as they are similarly informed about the informal powers of political parties and interest groups. Knowledge of these institutions might be superficial on the part of many, but citizens generally realize that parties and groups affect the substance of executive rulings, legislation, and even court decisions.

There is, however, another type of political institution that exists at each level of government; and it is far less understood by citizens and politicians alike. That institution is the bureaucracy, the administrative arm of the political system with its hundreds of bureaus and thousands of employees who serve as government's professional experts. This bureaucracy is closely tied to each of the other political institutions. The President, Governor, or Mayor is the bureaucracy's formal head, while the legislature shares control through its ability to appropriate or withhold

3

operating revenue. Likewise, courts have jurisdiction over bureau work, political parties attempt to secure top level bureau jobs and influential assignments for their members, and interest groups lobby bureaucrats just as they do legislators.

TABLE 1.1
THE UNITED STATES EXECUTIVE BRANCH BUREAUCRACY

EXECUTIVE OFFICE AGENCIES (10)

Central Administrative Unit	Office of Management and Budget
Council of Economic Advisors	Office of Science and Technology Policy
Council of Environmental Quality	Office of the Special Representative for Trade Negotiations
Council on Wage and Price Stability	National Security Council
Domestic Policy Staff	
Intelligence Oversight Board	

ADMINISTRATIVE DEPARTMENTS (13)

Agriculture	Health and Welfare	Labor
Commerce	Housing and Urban Development	State
Defense	Interior	Transportation
Education	Justice	Treasury
Energy		

INDEPENDENT ADMINISTRATIVE AGENCIES (82)

ACTION	General Service Administration
Agency for International Communication	National Aeronautics and Space Administration
Appalachian Regional Commission	National Science Foundation
Civil Aeronautics Board	Office of Personnel Management
Farm Credit Administration	Veterans Administration
Federal Deposit Insurance Corporation	And Others

Source: *Official Congressional Directory* (Washington, D.C.: U.S. Government Printing Office, 1977). Contains 1977-79 reorganizations.

Yet the bureaucracy is invisible and unknown to most Americans because it has no role to play in the big political spectaculars, the elections. The bureaucracy is not part of the political parties' efforts to win, control, and organize government through the ballot box. Bureaucrats are not forced to campaign or work for executive or legislative superiors in elections; and they cannot provide financial assistance from their treasuries the way interest groups do. Nor do they run for their offices themselves. All but a few top administrators gain their positions through merit examinations and specific job qualifications, and they are then

TABLE 1.2
A STATE BUREAUCRACY (MICHIGAN)

ADMINISTRATIVE DEPARTMENTS (21)

Agriculture	Education	Public Health
Attorney General	Labor	Social Service
Auditor General	Licensing and Regulation	State
Civil Rights	Management and Budget	State Highways
Civil Service	Mental Health	State Lottery
Commerce	Military Affairs	State Police
Corrections	Natural Resources	Treasury

INDEPENDENT ADMINISTRATIVE BUREAUS (31)

Bicentennial Commission	Great Lakes Commission
Commission on Indian Affairs	Drinking Driver Problem Task Force
Commission on Criminal Justice	Advisory Commission on Nutrition
Office of Economic Opportunity	And Others
Manpower Planning Council	
Women's Commission	

Source: *The Michigan Official Directory and Legislative Manual* (Lansing: Department of Administration, 1976).

TABLE 1.3
A CITY BUREAUCRACY (SAGINAW, MICHIGAN)

ADMINISTRATIVE DEPARTMENTS (10)

City Clerk	Fire	Parks and Recreation
Finance	Public Works and Engineering	Human Relations
Police	Health	
	Public Utilities	
	Community Development	

INDEPENDENT ADMINISTRATIVE BUREAUS (14)

Building Appeals	Housing Commission
Civic Center	Tri-City Airport
Economic Development Corporation	And Others
Fire Code	

Source: The City of Saginaw, 1977.

protected from dismissal by Civil Service regulations. As a result, these officials do not come and go when parties and elections reorder government. They remain on the job, providing continuity and stability to day-to-day political affairs. Therefore, bureaucratic organizations have rightfully been referred to as "independent establishments," operating apart from the frenzy of electoral politics.

There is much more to politics than elections and their direct results, however. Important decisions about the life and death of government programs are usually made away from the campaign trail and the candidate's platform. Executives and legislators need to know where to stand on specific issues and proposed solutions to problems, but elections seldom give them sufficient direction. Elections only place politicians in power, and then they must govern. This is where bureaucrats assume significance. They perform vital tasks in both the establishment and operation of public programs. As permanently employed professionals, bureaucrats frequently become the most important and influential participants in decisions made about programs because others rely on their expert advice and warnings on matters about which they lack first-hand knowledge.

This book is about the political decisions made by government bureaucrats. The intent is to illustrate their tremendous influence and show how and why they have it. There is explicitly a contention that bureaucrats at the bureau level normally have more impact than anyone else on the final allocation of program benefits. To some readers, this premise will seem odd or perhaps even preposterous. Most Americans still think of electoral activities as portrayed on television as the most crucial political events. Or they relate to Watergate-like deliberations matching President against Congress for extremely high stakes. On the other hand, the typical citizen hears the work "bureaucrat" and, if he knows what it means, immediately thinks of the license bureau clerk or a social worker. Bureaucracy conjures up images of red tape, burdensome regulations, and personal frustration from dealing with "those people." All of these visions present a biased and essentially incomplete view of how political decisions are made. Yet, as beliefs, they are understandable. Bureaucrats seldom get attention. They do not make their decisions in public, they are seldom followed by the press, and they need never be in the public eye to retain their jobs. Almost all their work goes on behind the scenes. For these reasons, this book is designed to meet its objectives by making bureaucrats and their political goals visible.

THE CLOAK OF BUREAUCRATIC INVISIBILITY

Before attempting to make bureaucrats more visible, however, some attention must be given to the underlying reason for their invisibility. And —if we go toward a common understanding of the rationale behind such problems as improper governmental oversight of bureaucracy, inattentive citizens, and nonparticipatory decision-making structures—there are not really a myriad of explanations. In fact, one tradition explains this bureaucratic condition, the classical orientation of administrative thought.

In the case of bureaucracy, like so much of life, the way people think about something begins to define its operation. After a consistent pattern of thought, a paradigm or model becomes established in the minds of most people in a society, accepting evidence or facts contrary to it is exceedingly difficult. As the father of American public administrative theory stated so precisely, "a social theory widely held by the actors has a self-confirming tendency and the classical theory is now engrained in our culture."[1] He means that citizens, elected politicians, and appointed bureaucrats share a belief in a bureaucratic ideal somewhat akin to what they already have. Or, at least, this ideal should be much like what already exists since they have jointly pursued such a bureaucratic goal for over one hundred years and, over that period, have consistently refined their bureaucracy to better meet the requirements of this ideal-type model.

The American bureaucratic model, and to some extent the model followed by all countries with developing administrative systems, follows the logic of the German organizational theorist, Max Weber.[2] In his writings, Weber developed the foundations for a rationally organized administrative structure in which formal rules and absolute legal principles would serve to order the behavior of those employed to carry out its assigned tasks. The bureaucracy would, therefore, be a servant of society. Or more specifically it would be a servant of society by responding directly to those who had the authority to control government—the elected representatives or royalty or whoever.

At the heart of Weber's model was the commitment to the belief that a governmental work unit could be established along purely technical lines. Such a unit would, in Weber's logic, necessarily be superior to any comparable unit brought together and operating on behalf of any personal loyalty or political rewards. The bureaucrat would do the correct thing neither because of coercion nor friendship but simply because of what the operating rules mandated.

According to Weber, such an ideal, rule-based organization would exhibit four essential characteristics regarding employee responsibility.

1. *Division of Labor.* The activities of the organization would be

divided into components according to the differing skills needed to complete the assignment. A caseworker in a social agency, for instance, would not need to prepare the agency's final budget. Responsibility for each assignment would be set by the rules of the organization and, where possible, by law. This prevents confusion on the part of employees and eliminates wasted time due to uncertainty.

2. *Autonomy of people and position.* Positions and assignments are to be defined only according to what jobs need be done, not according to who should do it. Thus, people are selected for a position on the basis of skill rather than the reverse, and human labor becomes an interchangeable commodity. "The job is permanent, the individual temporary."[3] People then only need be trained as specialists according to the way work is divided.

3. *Centralization of authority.* The organizational unit is established to ensure supervision and coordination. Each employee is watched to ensure correct completion of the assignment in order to make certain that all carefully designed assignments flow into the completion of the well-planned final product of the organization. Supervisory need is great, because if one employee fails the organization cannot succeed. As a result, at every stage in the work of the unit, there must be supervision; and a carefully defined hierarchy of superiors and subordinates becomes representative of the entire organization. Someone at the top must bear final responsibility for the finished product, for only at that point is the total assembly complete.

4. *Institutionalized record keeping.* Since rules serve as the operational principle of the organization and because supervisors exist to make sure the rules are followed, a vast amount of paperwork is necessarily generated. Without records of successful task completion, employees could not be rewarded. Without records of failure, employees could not be punished, nor could inadequate rules be improved upon. As a result, "red tape seems to be the blood line of bureaucracy."[4]

Weber's hoped for creation was the mechanization of human behavior and the greatest possible elimination of arbitrariness, error, sloth, and favoritism in the day-to-day operation of government. Those who assumed positions as employees were indeed to be nameless, faceless bureaucrats whose identities were unimportant because they were so easily replaceable. In other words, as people they were invisible.

Weber's theme easily fit the political problems of early twentieth-century American government. The corruption of political party machines was being attacked by reform-minded city residents bent on the elimination of patronage in employment and governance by long slates of elected officials. These reforms turned to merit hiring, the development of civil service, and the emergence of professional public administrators who were to protect government treasuries from party plunders and eliminate inequality in the distribution of public services. With the Progressive Movement the same logic and rationale was brought to state and federal government. Because of the common needs of the reformers and concerns of Weber, the machines of partisanship gave way to the orthodoxy of a machinelike bureaucracy. The politics of the time simply placed Weber's general theory of organization as a focal point for understanding the proper method of governmental operation. Eventually Weber slipped into place at the center of the dogma as more and more organizational theorists fell in line with his ideal-type model.

Frederick W. Taylor's theories of scientific management were especially notable in that Taylor's ideas addressed all organizations, not just the public sector.[5] In essence, Taylor claimed "one best way" existed for bringing about the production, completion, or provision of any good, product, service, or policy of the organization. Furthermore, Taylor argued that, like a machine, any human activity could be scientifically analyzed and measured to find that best method. Then technical adjustments could be made to the process in order to bring about the best performance. Because Taylor's ideas found widespread societal acceptance in general and since the reform forces of political change in particular were anxious to see government "run like a business," their adaptation to government was quick. Throughout the 1930's and 1940's the literature of public administration was absolutely dominated by methodologists advancing Taylor's management theory within Weber's ideal-type organization.

By necessity, bureaucrats were seen as such low level functionaries that, as individuals and as groups of people whose preferences and judgment counted, their existence hardly mattered. Government need not control them, theorists postulated; the machine could control itself and correct its own inefficiencies and errors. Citizens should not, in fact, become involved or share in decision-making because such participation would only detract from the machine's capability. By definition and through prescription, the organizational and governmental theorists of the time had to conclude that administration was distinct from politics. As they saw it and exclaimed, the two were separate processes.

POLITICS AND ADMINISTRATION AS ONE

"Administrators are continually laying down rules for the future," wrote Paul Appleby in 1949, "and administrators are continually determining what the law is, what it means in terms of action, what the rights of parties are with respect both to transactions in process and transactions in prospect."[6] Appleby's words were targeted against the prevailing Weberian orthodoxy, the distinction between politics and administration. He continued his debunking by noting that: "Administrators also participate in another way in the making of policy for the future; they formulate recommendations for legislation, and this is a part of the function of policy-making." Appleby concluded that it made little sense to separate the political decision from the administrative because both worked together to produce the benefits distributed by government. There was, in practice, no real line that distinguished between the two as the Weberian theorists contended. As Appleby points out, modern bureaucrats are not robots who complete tasks in a mechanized way. Instead they interpret, define, and plan for close working partners in other political institutions. And to do this work well they must be responsive, human, humane, and flexible.

As time has gone on, Appleby's wisdom has prevailed, and the distinction between politics and administration has been rejected, especially by students of public bureaucracy. The term "politics" has been generally accepted to define any and all behavior leading to the "authoritative allocation of values for a society."[7] Thus, the actions of the bureaucracy in providing advice and regulating affairs of state are considered political ones. And, as a result, bureaucracy is considered as one among many political institutions in America; and administration is but one kind of political activity.

This realization, however, has been slow. But it has come about because political participants have discovered that there can be no product of government that best satisfies or serves everyone. There is no definitively best product. Thus, there is no absolutely best way to determine what bureaucrats should produce and no best way to deliver each of their services. The world has too many customers, their demands are too diverse, and too many techniques must be employed to meet them for Weber's model to be real. Today's bureaucrats must address people as part of their decision-making, at least for the purposes of securing information.

In truth the bureaucracy is not really a single institution. It is an aggregate of many independent organizations that each have their own specialized jobs to perform for government relative to those different people they serve and products they provide. Like the term "government," the term "bureaucracy" has a collective meaning, not a singular one as Weber and Taylor would have us believe.

However, because of the legacy of Weber, Taylor, and their followers, much about the operation of bureaucracy derives from their theory. Especially significant is the relative anonymity of bureaucrats, even as their importance to society increases. While being politically involved, bureaucrats are expected to be neutral in their expressed feelings. While being active, they are not to be prominent as spokesmen for government. While make challenging recommendations, they are not to be acknowledged as leaders. Those are among the burdens with which American public administrators live. As the reader becomes familiar with bureaucracy throughout this book, it will become apparent that one of the most difficult of all assignments is for the politically involved bureaucrat to meet society's Weberian expectations.

WHAT IS "BUREAUCRACY"?

There are many ways to refer to "bureaucracy" in American politics. For instance, there is the federal, or national government's bureaucracy, which is usually considered to be the thirteen departments, ten presidential offices, and eighty independent agencies under the control of the President as Chief Administrator.[8] However, the definition of "federal bureaucracy" could be expanded by also considering the many other separate organizations responsible to the President and listed in a separate category of the *United States Government Manual* as "Selected Boards, Committees and Commissions."[9] Or one might include the six administrative organizations of the Congress, the Federal Judicial Center, and the Administrative Office of the United States Courts as part of the federal bureaucracy. Then too, all of the states and all of the larger local governments have bureaucracies of their own which are not part of the federal bureaucracy. And, since considerable intergovernmental activity exists which brings national, state, and local bureaucrats together for common purposes, it is appropriate to refer to a comprehensive "American public bureaucracy."

It should be clear that the term "bureaucracy" as used here refers only to the general position that an administrative organization occupies as a part of a government. Specifically, it is an abstract term and is not used as a name for the actual bureaucratic units that are involved in politics. Those units are called *bureaus*, and they are the places where expert decisions are made and where political action takes place.[10]

Bureaus are created through the authority of the legislature, usually as part of a bill authorizing government intervention in a particular area of social or economic unrest. For example, the Economic Development Administration was established by the Public Works and Economic

Development Act of 1964 when it was decided that unemployment in certain economically distressed sections of the nation had to be dealt with. In some instances, the chief executive, with legislative consent, can authorize the creation of a bureau while reorganizing his administration. The Office of Environmental Sciences began this way as part of President Nixon's Reorganization Plan 3 of 1970.

When bureaus are created, they are given certain general responsibilities to perform called *missions*. The mission of the Office of Environmental Sciences is to exercise responsibility for "research, development, and demonstration activities in the areas of criteria development, establishment of environmental quality standards, and location of control activities."[11] The identification of such a mission charges the bureau with the responsibility of developing expertise in a specific area. From that point on, until the executive and legislature agree to abolish it, the bureau works to propose solutions to any problems that arise in its area of responsibility.

The workload of the bureau is divided according to the *programs* it is authorized to operate. Programs are the specific assignments that allow the bureau to undertake tasks within its area of expertise after problems have been identified. Constructing houses, distributing welfare funds, regulating public utility rates and the like are all specified in the programs that the legislature passes to allow bureaus these powers.

The major constraint placed on the bureau is its funding. Bureaus normally are allocated a certain number of dollars for each fiscal year for each of their programs plus general operating revenue. These funds allow the bureau to house itself, hire employees, purchase supplies, purchase materials for programs, disperse direct payments to clients, and travel for investigative purposes. Both total revenue and the funds allocated to specific programs are subject to review by both the executive and the legislature during the annual process of government budgeting. Even though a bureau might be authorized to spend funds several years into the future, their operating capital is technically subject to yearly scrutiny if the budgeters desire to reconsider. This makes it mandatory for the bureau to prepare an annual summary report of its accomplishments and expenditures for their consideration.

The assignment of government programs for research and implementation, the ability to spend allocated funds on programs, and the authorization to employ skilled personnel to do the work distinguishes bureaus from other government institutions. Neither elected officials nor the courts have the authority to engage in these enterprises. Only bureaus do. However, bureaus are not all given that formal title in every instance. Many of the organizations that act as "bureaus" are officially known as "agencies," "divisions," "authorities," "task forces," "services," "offices," "foundations," "corporations," "commissions," "institutes," and "departments." Such titles often seem to depend on little more than whim, but they certainly do confuse observers as to the identity of the organization.

This situation is made more complicated by the fact that most bureaus are created as a part of other administrative organizations whose job it is to assist in their supervision. For example, the Bureau of Health Insurance is contained in the Social Security Administration, which in turn is part of the Department of Health, Education and Welfare. Similarly, the Bureau of Libraries and Learning Resources is part of the Office of Higher Education within the Office of Education which is also within HEW. Bureaus like Health Insurance or Libraries and Learning Resources are the important organizations to understand because they are the ones that operate programs and use government funds and manpower to directly affect the citizenry. The supervisory organizations are important as referees but lack the direct political prominence of bureaus.

Even that generalization is far too simplified. In practice, the Social Security Administration, the Office of Education, or HEW itself could operate programs of their own without establishing a subordinate bureau. In fact, many organizations actually engage in both supervision and program operation. However, in that case, it must be remembered that they are operating as bureaus as an important part of their workload.

Illustration 1.1 should give the reader an indication of the vast number of bureaus in the public bureaucracy—and it refers to one of the smallest of the federal departments, Justice. All of the units listed as "boards," "commissions," and "bureaus" operate as bureaus with ongoing programs providing goods and services to clients outside the Justice Department. The units titled "offices" also act as bureaus, but their programs provide staff assistance to other bureaus and supervisory organizations within the Justice Department. In all, 22 bureaus are included in that one department. It should be kept in mind that there are 50 states and over 80,000 municipalities, counties, townships, and special districts in the United States. None of them operate as many bureaus as the approximately 1,900 of the federal government, yet anyone's mind would boggle if they were added up.

The vast number of bureaus is easily understood if one reflects on their assignments and responsibilities. Bureaus have become government's resident specialists on various societal problems (i.e., higher education, health insurance, disease control, aging, etc.). Potential problem areas are divided up, and the bureaus become the knowledgeable experts responsible for each. This division of labor, following the logic but not the task orientation of Weber, is the only way government can cope with

ILLUSTRATION 1.1

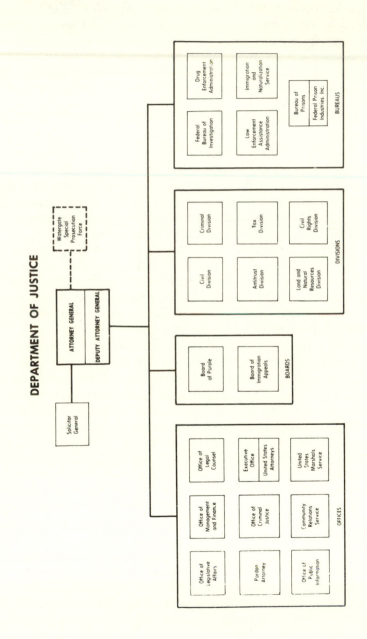

the increasingly large, complex, and technological society which constantly makes more demands for services.[12] Therefore, it makes sense that bureaus proliferate and exist in great abundance. But it also makes it extremely difficult for citizens in general to identify and keep track of the many sources of the goods and services that bureaus provide.

BUREAU ACTIVITY

Government's job, it is often said, is to *make policy*. The negotiated settlement between the United States and the Soviet Union, for instance, established a policy of détente between those two countries. Détente, as negotiated, meant that the United States government agreed to work for friendly relations and mutual cooperation with the Soviets. However, the policy of détente did not spell out specific tasks for the U.S. government to perform, nor did it commit funds for specified policy goals. Those responsibilities were left to bureaus and the programs they could design to further U.S.-Soviet cooperation. One of the bureaus that played an important part was the Foreign Agricultural Service when it arranged a program for sales of American wheat to Russia.

Although bureaus are not direct policy-makers, policy would be impossible without them. That is because "policy" describes only the general guidelines, or goals, that give direction to specific programs. By itself, policy is no more than a goal, a hoped-for end or result.[13] Agricultural policy, for example, aims at the expansion of crop production. But it is impossible to understand or predict what government will do to obtain this or any other policy goal just by knowing about the existence of the policy. In order to understand agricultural policy, it is necessary to examine the net effect of several programs, including ones which provide subsidy supports to farmers, others which encourage them to grow certain crops, and a third type restricting the acreage planted to any one commodity.

The organizational division of labor within the bureaucracy makes it very difficult for bureaus to strive for consistency in coordinating all pertinent programs. Typically, as is the case in the agricultural example above, different bureaus are responsible for the different programs. Although the Agriculture Department's job is to supervise bureau activity and help resolve differences between programs, a group of related programs often fails to do everything necessary to obtain policy goals. Sometimes programs will even be working at cross-purposes with one another. (See Illustration 1.2.) This is because bureaus are requested to pay heed to policies but are organized with their narrow missions as their principal concern. Bureaus exist to deal with problems unique to their own limited expertise. They are assigned only programs related to their specialized knowledge. And, if they are shortsighted or develop narrow interests as a result, it is quite understandable.

Supervisory departments and agencies do not assign programs based on which bureau will best meet policy goals. Assignments are made on the basis of specialization. The Bureau of Higher Education does not,

ILLUSTRATION 1.2

AN EXAMPLE OF BUREAU JURISDICTION

THE FOLLOWING EXCHANGE ALLEGEDLY TOOK PLACE BETWEEN STAFF OF THE ENVIRONMENTAL PROTECTION AGENCY AND AN INTERVIEWER FROM HARPER'S WEEKLY

EPA: Good morning, EPA press office.
HW: I'd like to know what you're doing about the ozone problem.
EPA: What ozone problem?
HW: The problem of aerosol spray propellants releasing chlorine atoms in the upper atmosphere that will break down vast amounts of ozone and destroy life on earth.
EPA: Can I call you back?
    * * *
HW: Good afternoon, Harper's Weekly.
EPA: Yes, this is the EPA in Washington calling with regard to your inquiry.
HW: Yes?
EPA: I just want to know, are you concerned about vinyl chloride?
HW: No, ozone.
EPA: Okay, I'll call you back.
    * * *

EPA: Good morning, EPA press office.
HW: Yes, EPA, I called last week and the week before. I was just wondering if you ever found out about the ozone problem?
EPA: Oh, yes. I thought I got back to you.
HW: No, you didn't. What's the EPA doing about it?
EPA: You don't want the EPA, that's not our area. You want the National Oceanic and Atmospheric Administration. They handle the upper atmosphere.
HW: But what about the danger of aerosol propellants to the future of life on earth?
EPA: I'm sorry. We just handle pollution.

SOURCE: HARPER'S WEEKLY 64 (JANUARY 10, 1975), P. 1

---

for instance, give grants to elementary schools through the Office of Education. Those programs and problem areas are under the administrative jurisdiction of the Bureau of Elementary and Secondary Education, and programs will be theirs. Exceptions occur only rarely when considerable overlap exists between two bureaus. In other instances, bureaus enjoy monopoly control over programs related to their expertise and mission.

Defense policy provides another illustration. This policy is determined by various national needs in the areas of attack prevention, first strike capability, limited armed might, technical production, energy, economic welfare, and, perhaps, environmental protection. But careful examination shows that no military bureau concerns itself with all of these problems. The latter three are not even of much concern to the total Defense Department, let alone one of its operational bureaus. Therefore, defense policy, if it is even to be discussed with regard to the bureaucracy, must be seen as a hodge-podge of programs, each assigned to diverse units. The bureaus may work to effect policy, but they do so by stressing the contributions of their own programs. In a situation like this there is no assurance that balanced policy guidelines will even exist, because defense policy is determined by whatever capabilities various programs offer. And capabilities are a result of bureaus working on the programs to which they are most committed.

The unanswered question is: What do bureaus do with governmental programs? The explanation must be a qualified one. On some programs, bureaus do almost everything; on others, they do very little. But, to at least some extent, bureaus *develop, implement,* and *evaluate* programs. And in so doing they establish *regulations* which dictate how the program will be operated and how its goods and services will be used by recipients.

Program development means planning for what will be done. And, since government programs are attacks on specific problems, it means that someone must prepare and design the assault. This is usually done, at least in part, by government bureaus. Sometimes bureau officials begin work at the request of the President, Congress, or a bureaucratic superior. Perhaps even more often, because bureaus must be attentive to occurrences within their areas of expertise, they begin on their own. After all, bureaus are the acknowledged source of government information, and being aware of changing conditions in order to alert others is one reason for their existence.

Planning brings several responsibilities to the bureau which are routine steps for any new program. In the first phase of development, bureaus organize themselves internally to prepare for their task. Then they become fact finders who appraise societal conditions and gather data as indicators of existing needs. This is essentially a research role, and it extends into a second phase, assembling the information. Facts seldom stand by themselves. Bureau personnel must assemble and interpret facts for other political participants such as the President or a legislator who will use the data in debating the need for a program.

Usually interpretation involves recommending what kind of action the government should take. If a bureau recommends a new program, its officials are the ones most likely to actually draft, or write up, the bill brought before the legislature. But, regardless of who drafts the bill, bureau officials normally will follow through and advocate their recommendations until they become law or are rejected.

Program implementation occurs after the legislation has been passed, and it also involves a great deal of planning. As with development, it follows its own routines. Additional planning is necessitated by the form that legislation usually takes. Programs are passed and put into effect through enabling legislation, or *enabling acts.*These are generally no more than outlines of what is to be done to accomplish the program's intent. Enabling acts contain the program's basic provisions and provide general direction for the bureau assigned to carry it out. For example, a bill authorizing the Law Enforcement Assistance Administration to award special revenue sharing funds would list such things as the total amount of expenditures, the purpose of the legislation, the priorities to be funded in light of that purpose, and the types of agencies eligible to receive funds.

This means that the bureau, or LEAA in this case, still must plan for the actual disbursement of the funds after the law is passed. To do this, they must decide independently what types of requests fit the priorities. Then they must find methods for judging how likely it is that particular requests will meet the goals of the enabling act. The bureau must also spell out such things as which organizations are eligible to receive funds, what characteristics determine eligibility, and what conditions the recipients must agree to meet. This means that bureaus need to plan additional requirements, or regulations, which are appended to the enabling act so as to make the program available to society.

The authority to regulate while implementing programs is the one formal power of the bureau. Regulations allow various bureaus to do such things as set rates for public utilities, determine who can sell stocks and bonds, require citizen participation in planning for the construction of public housing, and prevent the manufacture of combustion engines which pollute beyond a predetermined level. These rules are determined by the bureau as a result of its research and, in effect, they allow bureau officials to control the behavior of those to whom the program applies. However, regulatory power extends beyond rule-making. Bureaus also *interpret* how regulations apply to specific cases; and they *adjudicate*, or serve as the original judge and jury, when their interpretive rulings are challenged. If those who are affected by regulations disagree with either the regulation or its application, their appeals go to the bureau and then, under certain conditions, to bureaucratic superiors before they have access to the courts.

The final task of the bureau is program evaluation. In evaluating programs, bureaus determine the success or failure of what they've done. This means that more facts must be gathered, assembled, and interpreted.

And it means that the bureau must find a method to determine whether its program has accomplished its goal of correcting a previously identified problem. Bureau officials try to discover how conditions would have changed without their program. Then the program is justified to other political forces if the information warrants its continuation. Or, modification and changes are proposed, and the evaluation process merges into a new stage of program development.

Development, implementation, and evaluation are not usually distinct processes.[14] Bureaus develop programs with an eye to implementation because they realize that assignments will normally be made to the agency arranging the plan. In addition, few programs are ever so successful that they need no modification. Even successful programs confront new situations and both operations and regulations must be modified. The work of the bureau is never finished, and after it becomes an established organization the bureau is never restricted to involvement with new programs. As a result, each bureau must always live with its past in preparing its future.

BUREAUS NEVER WORK ALONE

The process of putting a program into effect never involves just the bureau. This is especially true for those bureaus which operate programs for use outside the organization. Legislators and interest group representatives are included at various stages when their concerns are affected. The department or agency to which the bureau belongs, the government's budgeting office, and, at least on major issues, its chief executive also participate in decisions affecting the program. This obviously complicates things. Each of these participants has his own concerns and preferences. Their views will be similar in many respects but their diverse interests will cause them to differ on many features of the program. This results in political conflict and, usually, compromises where participants "split their differences" on common points where they meet and disagree.

The compromises resulting from this interaction are determined by the ability of the participants to make one another perceive their own importance. A governor may show that he can successfully veto a bill; or a legislator can demonstrate that his amendment will carry. This is *political influence,* and the impact the various participants have on the program is a measure of how much they possess. Bureaucrats have a great amount of influence in the American political system. Presidents and congressmen may say "yes" or "no" to a program. Interest groups can lobby for or against it. Or the courts might even rule it unconstitutional. But only the bureau nurtures the program along from conception until the time it becomes a reality; and only the bureau has day-to-day ability to regulate a program's users. Individuals within Congress or the White House might actually have conceived the need for a program and written its enabling legislation; but, in most cases, bureau cooperation facilitated their work.[15] Those things are what make bureaus politically influential.

Influence is derived from the *resources* that participants bring to the political scene. Interest groups, for instance, have influence with a congressman when they can show him that the group is composed of a large number of citizens who will cast their votes the way their lobbyist dictates. The people and the votes they represent are both political resources and result in the interest group having some control over the legislator. Such organizations seldom stop there in making their presence felt by other political participants. They also work to increase the prestige of their members, organize more effective methods for delivering campaign funds and information to decision-makers, develop better strategies for being heard, and, generally, do anything else that might give them an increased advantage in the political process.[16] Prestige, organization, strategy; all of these are resources which can gain influence if used correctly. Bureaus are no exception. The successful accomplishment of their goals is dependent on the resources they can demonstrate and apply.

The major resource of a bureau comes from its expertise in planning. Because of its fact-finding and research skills, the bureau is potentially able to supply answers to politicians involved in problem areas related to the bureau's jurisdiction, and almost all politicians depend on such information in their jobs. For example, the President needs information before he can recommend a proposal to Congress. If the President does not appear knowledgeable and informed about the subject at hand, congressmen will not listen to his directives. Instead, they will challenge him and propose changes they prefer. This was clearly evident in late 1974 as Senate Majority Leader Mike Mansfield and others challenged President Ford on his "Whip Inflation Now" proposals. They did not believe that the President knew best, and the criticism of Ford by various dissenting bureaucrats further undermined the President's credibility. He looked like a man without the answers and was, therefore, unable to muster additional supporters to rally against Congress. Ford's reliance on his laissez-faire economic beliefs led to such increased disenchantment that a *New York* magazine cover portrayed him with a "WIN" button and a painted clown face.[17] This dramatic statement summarized what many politicians thought of his knowledge and leadership capability.

Likewise, congressmen need facts and information to get the respect and ear of their legislative colleagues. And, because of the norms of trust and reciprocity within the legislature, their ability to get others to listen to them and respond is one of the legislature's major resources.[18] Most of

ILLUSTRATION 1.3

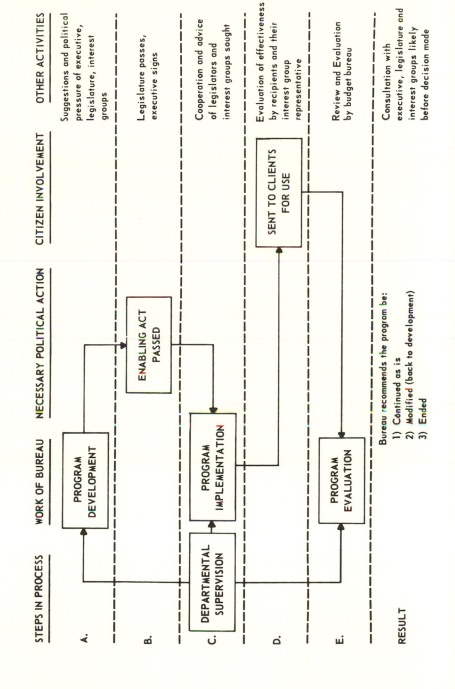

PROGRAM STEPS IN THE BUREAUCRATIC PROCESS AND RELATED ACTIVITIES

this information, as is also the case with the President, must be obtained from the bureaus because elected officials usually lack the time, energy, and research skills to obtain it on their own. The result is that most politicians foster bureau ties in order to be effective in their other relationships.

For this reason, almost all political participants treat some bureaus as a valuable ally *as long as the bureau can and will be of assistance.* When alliances develop, bureau officials provide what help they can in return for (1) deference to their judgment and (2) support in obtaining new programs and increased funding. This is especially likely to be true when politicians use the bureau on a regular basis and get to know its officials well.[19] Regular interaction of this sort often occurs because of the specialization of congressional committee members, interest groups, and even presidential assistants. The same people tend to be interested in housing problems or those of mass transit, nuclear defense, or water pollution each time these problems come up. Accordingly, it makes sense to develop informal relationships based upon mutual assistance, trust, and cooperation because all of these individuals know they will be working with one another time after time.

Situations of this sort make it imperative for the bureau to be a good source of information. It also means that the bureau must constantly concern itself with *its ability to help others.* This is the most marketable resource it has at its disposal for exercising political influence. Others can actually pass legislation, use their formal authority to direct change, or bring electoral pressure. But the bureau must reply primarily on its specialized expertise to secure its needs.

A bureau has one other important resource, control over the implementation of programs. But, implementation normally does not provide as much strength as that which comes from the bureau's ability to provide information. In practice, bureaus can regulate or otherwise implement programs to serve some clients better than others or please one politician especially well. A bomber squadron might be assigned to a particular congressman's district, generating economic opportunities for his constituents back home. Or a water reservoir might be built in one state rather than another because of a senator's committee assignment. Likewise, eligibility requirements contained in the provisions of a housing program could be shifted to a higher income level. This would allow the bureau to placate or bargain with an interest group whose support is needed or a congressman who believes that middle-class families need greater opportunities for governmental assistance.

At first glance, such exchanges seem like a potent source of bureau influence. But discretion in implementing programs does not bring as much strength to the bureau as its ability to provide information. The bureau, in actuality, must be quite cautious in distributing its rewards because its closest and regular supporters must be pleased first. Otherwise, their assistance might not be continued with past enthusiasm. Thus, bureaus normally use such opportunities to solidify previously established relationships. Oftentimes the bureau actually consults with its supporters and makes decisions with their political needs in mind. For instance, a decision on the reservoir location or housing provision might be left to a congressional ally. The congressman, in turn, can bargain as he pleases with this decision in order to further his own purposes within the legislature. All of which removes much of the bureau's discretion in dealing with others, but bureau officials willingly cooperate because they realize that regular allies must remain happy if they are to remain allies.

Regular supporters, to a degree, become an additional, although indirectly controlled, resource of the bureau since they can be counted on for assistance. These individuals can, depending on who they are, win legislative votes for a new program, convince the President and Office of Management and Budget of the value of increased funding, or stop another interest group's assault on the bureau. The bureau uses its resources to gain friends who will then go out and use their influence to assist the bureau. Such friends are willing to help because they realize that much of their own political strength comes from the bureau.

This all means that bureaus are never really politically independent in their concern with programs. Each bureau must always be calculating both its own resources and the extent of its reliance on other political participants who can affect its ability to function. As a result, much bureaucratic activity must be understood in terms of the need to gain and hold allies from other important political institutions. Bureaus are not just engaged in looking for better answers to societal problems and regulating the resulting programs. They are also preoccupied with fitting into the political process as valued partners of other active participants.

BUREAUCRATS

It should be obvious that the license bureau clerk who was mentioned earlier is not the civil servant who is the subject of this book. Clerical employees and maintenance workers surely have their place in government, but they wield little or no political influence. Stories are often told of the secretary who keeps the office running smoothly, despite the boss. However, these tales are usually overdone. The secretary seldom makes crucial decisions about government programs. So individuals of this type mean very little to bureaucratic politics.

That does not mean, however, that top level management officials are the only politically significant bureau personnel. On the contrary, a majority of bureau employees fall into the influential category. These include bureau chiefs, middle managers, and lower-ranking researchers with responsibility for portions of a program. All of these individuals are appointed to governmental positions on the basis of their potential for performing specific tasks. Some of them have general administrative skills, but even more are professional and technical specialists who design and operate programs. Such individuals, in fact, outnumber the general administrators by nearly 19 to 1 in the federal bureaucracy, and they are the ones who provide the answers which become the bureau's political resources.[20]

Engineers, botanists, and social scientists do as much or more program development work as project specialists or logistic support personnel. These same individuals work with computer technicians and auditors to evaluate bureau accomplishments. Programs could never be implemented without police officers, social workers, teachers, and other "street-level bureaucrats" who also contribute by reporting on programmatic successes and failures.

It is important to remember that specialists dominate bureau operations. Even the managers must gain special acquaintance and familiarity with bureau programs to survive in their positions. It is no longer sufficient to "work well with people" or "know numbers" in order to manage a program. Administrators, professionals, and technicians alike must gain a first-hand knowledge of programmatic needs before they can effectively proceed with their specialized assignments.

To some extent, specialized knowledge has always been a prerequisite for bureau operations. Specialists were always assigned to operate the army or build the roads. But a larger, more complex, and more technical world confronts government and bureaucracy today. Bureaucrats, as a result, are expected to know more about their problem areas, and training requirements have steadily gone up.

The pre-1930's public bureaucracy, in either size or skill, bears little resemblance to the one that now exists. Few World War II era officials would, in fact, recognize today's bureaucracy. Bureaus and bureaucrats emerged so rapidly at all levels of American government that, at times in the 1950's and 1960's, public employment was the fastest growing segment of the economy. More politicians were being hired every day; and they brought expertise, political resources, and political influence to their bureaus.

These hired politicians also brought, as they still do today, additional perspectives to their work.[21] All of them are complex persons with many nonprofessional goals which differentiate them from their colleagues. As bureau officials, these people project their own social and other political identities into decision-making. For instance, a staunch Republican in the National Park Service might try to resist the intrusion of a Democratic congressman, even if he does rely on him for funds. Similarly, that bureaucrat might go out of his way to cooperate with a Republican President. His partisan identity gives him more than the average desire to listen to that particular chief executive. Interest group identification operates the same way. It is safe to conclude that an active and lifelong member of the American Farm Bureau Federation would give a very sympathetic hearing to that group were it to appear before him in the Agriculture Marketing Service or Farmers Home Administration. A consumer's union or the National Association of Manufacturers would be unlikely to receive such a cordial greeting when lobbying there.

Social identities are no less important. A conservative Catholic might oppose any of his bureau's programs which aid abortions. Or an official of the Public Health Service might give special consideration to burn treatment grants because of an accident to a child or wife. Any number of possibilities exist which can bias a bureaucrat to favor one program or solution over another.

These human factors make it very difficult to predict what a bureau's proposals will be. But, to a great extent, such considerations are not as crucial to the outcome of decisions as they might be. The environment employees face within the bureau is the one common denominator that unites most personnel within a shared interest.[22] At work, the bureau becomes the prime source of identification as the individual wrestles with its problems.[23]

Obviously, common identification is not universal, and all bureaucrats continue to have somewhat different personal orientations. However, no one can forget the necessity of justifying his proposals and protecting the bureau's political resources. His funds and job depend on it. Bureaucrats are protected from interfering politicians by the merit system, but they still lose their employment if their programs get no support. Promotions, pensions, and their quality of life are tied to the successfulness of their programs. Bureaucrats normally count on the security of their jobs. They intend to stay as public employees. Therefore, although officials may differ, the good of the bureau is always kept carefully in mind by all of them.

The following chapters will pay a great amount of attention to the job related self-interest of bureaucrats. It cannot be assumed that the officials who make a bureau's decisions have the best interest of the society as their guiding philosophy. They are too closely wedded to their programs for one to accept that belief. The facts of political life lead to another conclusion.

Bureau recommendations almost never propose budget cuts, an end to one of their programs, or abolishment of their bureau. It is possible to examine government records for months without finding proposals of this sort, especially the latter. This leads to the belief that it is always necessary to suspect bureau officials of operating so as to serve their own narrow interests.

SUMMARY

Governmental activity, or politics, affects the goods people value by offering solutions to societal problems. The solutions, when they require government action, take the form of programs that must be paid for and worked on. But these programs are not easily put into operation. They require careful research and specialized planning that only expert, but at the same time self-interested, government employees can provide. These officials belong to bureaus; and the responsibility for program development, implementation, and evaluation is assigned there. This involvement makes the bureaucrat a potentially influential political participant who also has the day-to-day ability to regulate all the goods and services government provides. In fact, bureaucrats are just as consequential to political decisions as any of the elected officials or interest group representatives with whom they must interact. And bureaus have an amount of regulatory discretion that makes them as powerful and independent as any other political institution. Yet, as people, bureaucrats are largely invisible, and much about the operation of government ensures that they attempt to retain their anonymity.

So far these points have been made in the abstract or by citing specific illustrations. Because bureaus are so unfamiliar to most people, each point deserves further elaboration in a more detailed fashion. The next chapter examines, in detail, one bureau of the federal government.

2...

THE BUREAU of MINES
at WORK

The Bureau of Mines (BOM) is an excellent example of an organization hidden in the institutional maze of American politics. Probably few citizens have ever heard its name. Yet BOM is an old and established bureau, one of twenty-eight located within the United States Department of Interior (DOI). The bureau is also politically prominent, although no one would ever think so if prominence were equated with political visibility. But because the responsibilities of BOM constitute only a small percentage of the dozens assigned to the Department of Interior, it is easy for political observers to overlook the bureau by concentrating on the "big picture" of United States interior problems or the controversial issues within the department. Such issues as Indian rights or the harvesting of trees from national forests normally gain most public attention.

The Department of Interior is divided into four major jurisdictional areas: Fish and Wildlife and Parks, Energy and Minerals, Land and Water Resources, and Indian Affairs. Individual offices within the departmental structure supervise all bureaus within each area. The Bureau of Mines, along with nine other bureaus, falls under the supervision of the Office of Energy and Minerals. (See Illustration 2.1.) However, only two of the nine, the Mining Enforcement and Safety Administration and the Office of Minerals Policy Development, have responsibilities that are closely related to BOM. The overall jurisdictions of the Interior Department and the Office of Energy and Minerals are both so broad in scope that widely disparate bureaus with almost no common grounds for interaction are organized together for supervisory purposes.

Departmental responsibilities range from the sociological problems of Native American reservation life to the technical aspects of power dam

ILLUSTRATION 2.1

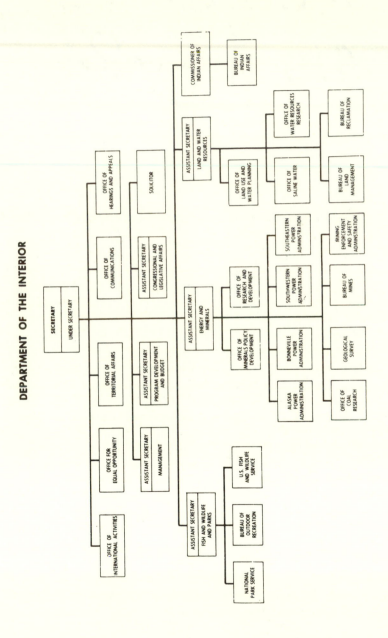

DEPARTMENT OF THE INTERIOR

operation. Its concerns include aesthetic problems of scenic preservation as well as planning for human survival through clean water research. In addition, DOI has responsibility for the political, social, and economic development of American territories. The Office of Energy and Minerals has "the authority and direct responsibility for programs associated with mineral data and analysis; generation, transmission, and marketing of electric power . . . ; mine health, safety, and training programs, topographic, geological, and mineral resource matters; energy, metallurgical, and mining research and development; and emergency preparedness and natural disaster, energy and minerals functions." And the office "is responsible for the development and coordination of ocean minerals resources affairs."[1] This great variety of assignments makes it extremely difficult for either the department or office to comparatively assess the effectiveness, worth, and needs of the many programs under its formal control.

The number of bureaus that independently operate DOI programs further complicates supervision and comparison. In all, twenty-one of the bureaus within DOI operate their own programs for use by clients outside the department. These include all the bureaus within the four major offices plus the Offices of Territorial Affairs and International Activities.

There are, additionally, a number of bureaus that provide staff support programs to assist the internal coordination of the department and the operations of the other bureaus. These include the other seven bureaus and, to some extent, the Office of International Activities as well. Of these bureaus, several are of particular importance to the Bureau of Mines. The Office of Congressional and Legislative Affairs and the Office of Management, Program Development and Budget attempt to assist in departmental supervision of BOM programs. But they also provide technical and management aid which is frequently of great assistance to the bureau. Similarly BOM gains legal and regulatory assistance from the Solicitor's Office and the Office of Hearings and Appeals. On balance, these support bureaus do little to remove the independence that the bureau enjoys from other organizations within the department even though some uniform procedures and policy guidelines are imposed. If anything, these bureaus remove some administrative burdens from BOM and allow its personnel to focus attention on their own clients, special problems, and research interests.

ITS MISSION

From a bureau standpoint, the mission of the Bureau of Mines is comparably as broad as the responsibilities of its department and office. According to the provisions of the enabling legislation establishing BOM, the Organic Act of 1910, the bureau was mandated "to conduct inquiries and . . . investigations concerning mining, and the preparation, treatment, and utilization of mineral substances with a view to improving health conditions, and increasing safety, efficiency, economic development, and conserving resources . . . to investigate explosives . . . and to disseminate information concerning these subjects.[2] Over the years, interpretations of this act by both Congress and the executive branch brought about a variety of programs firmly establishing the Bureau of Mines as the U.S. government's resident expert on all matters of mining technology, metallurgy, energy, and mineral resources. In the orthodox view of federal officials, if a substance was nonliving and came from within the earth, it was under the jurisdiction of BOM. And, if a problem arose concerning any of these substances, it was for the bureau to resolve.

As a result of its broad responsibilities regarding mining, minerals, metals, and energy sources, BOM operates some very significant and costly federal programs. For example, the recycling of solid wastes, oil shale processing, and the conversion of industry from coal to cleaner fuels are all bureau programs. On a more routine level, the bureau is undertaking several programs to increase mining productivity, the efficiency of extracting oil and gas, and American capabilities to withstand changes in the international availability of natural resources. While all these efforts are clearly identified with BOM's mission, other responsibilities have frequently been assigned there or requested by bureau officials when no other bureau was readily equipped for them. For instance, the Bureau of Mines has been responsible for the production and sale of helium gases and for research into the environmental hazards associated with mineral extraction and use.

During its first sixty years, BOM demonstrated increased growth in each of the areas noted in its mission except safety.[3] Until 1969 and passage of the Federal Coal Mine Health and Safety Act, that whole subject was left to token efforts, campaign speeches, and the promises of industry. However, when it became clear that U.S. mine safety was far below that of several more safety-conscious nations, the Bureau of Mines began to take its safety mission more seriously. Since that time, BOM has developed several programs to improve working conditions and practices, prevent accidents, and minimize occupational diseases in industries extracting or developing resources within the bureau's jurisdiction.

The two major features characterizing Bureau of Mines's activities can be seen by reviewing the vast array of its programs. The bureau has never had a single focus or resource concern to direct its own efforts toward. With regard to possible subjects for investigation, the bureau has covered the range of extractive industries and resources. Second, with only a few exceptions, BOM has not concerned itself with programs that could be operated internally by the bureau alone. Its programs have always been ventures dependent on privately owned extractive industries for final implementation. As a result of these two factors, the broad, diversified mission of the Bureau of Mines has been carried out with only one end in mind. For over sixty-five years, the bureau has been little more than an assistant for those private industries providing mineral and fuel needs for the nation.

RESEARCH

BOM's role in stimulating private enterprise should not be surprising. The United States has obvious vital needs in the areas administered by the bureau; and periodic supply shortages have made it evident to federal officials that government intervention and oversight are both necessary and proper. At the same time, American ideology and traditions have limited this intervention short of public control of any of the extractive industries. Nationalization similar to the British takeover of coal mines has been unthinkable in the United States; and federal experimentation with privately controlled operations has been viewed by industrial managers as too burdensome. The presence of on-site BOM officials and their experiments, business owners agree, interferes with production and business activities.

With those options closed, and with a need to demonstrate its value, the Bureau of Mines evolved as a service-oriented organization. Two types of service have been emphasized: *market assistance* and *R & D*, or the research and development of technological innovations in extraction and production.

Although the bureau does not directly promote the sale of natural resources, its data network provides invaluable information to the operators, owners, and investors of extractive industries. BOM "collects, compiles, analyzes, and publishes data" about the "exploration, production, shipment, demand, stocks, prices, imports, and exports" of all commodities under its jurisdiction. And it makes important projections not only about resource consumption and availability, but also regarding the effects of potential developments in the economy, technology, international affairs and legal rulings."[4]

The bureau's R & D activities are more extensive than its market analysis and forecasting. Most research and development goes on in eighteen field research centers maintained for the exclusive use of BOM. There are four mining centers, six centers for energy programs, and eight others for metallurgical research. The relatively high number of centers reflects the decentralized operation of the bureau as well as its need to conduct experimental research close to areas of extraction and production. Thus, mining centers are found in such locations as Denver and Spokane, while fossil fuel research is carried out in places like Morgantown, West Virginia, and Laramie, Wyoming.

All of the research centers are multipurpose complexes with several experimental stations and a wide range of administrative offices supplementing those in BOM's Washington headquarters. In addition to their more traditional laboratories and testing facilities, these stations also contain productive mines and plants. For example, the Pittsburg Energy Research Center operates a Synthane Pilot Plant for producing substitute natural gas from coal, and the College Park, Maryland, Metallurgy Research Center constructed a plant to test the feasibility of converting garbage to usable fuel. Similar kinds of experimental projects are operated by the centers at still other sites when, for political or practical reasons, center locations provide an inadequate environment for testing. A recently constructed example is an experimental pilot plant at Kellogg, Idaho, where conditions encourage research in air quality standards.

Despite this diversity of location and purpose, research within the bureau is more coordinated than it might appear. The mining, energy, and metallurgy research divisions are directed by headquarters personnel who monitor, budget, and assist in the staffing of the various centers. And headquarters personnel under the director's office must examine and approve all programs and major changes even though they neither direct nor control any of them. As a result, no centers are autonomous organizations.

The bureau's division of labor also provides procedures for administrative review before any programs become operative. All newly proposed programs are examined in detail because of the bureau's distinction between *pure* and *applied* research. Employees doing pure or basic research are looking for new ideas or technical breakthroughs in their areas of interest; while the applied projects are organized to determine what previous discoveries from pure research either mean or offer. For purposes of conducting research, BOM sites all have a rather stable budget for pure research and are allocated additional funds when newly generated innovations need to be advanced to the applied stage. But before these funds are received and a new program becomes a reality, all requests are, at least in theory, scrutinized by personnel from the divisions, administration, the bureau director's office, the Office of Energy and Minerals, the Department, and finally, the Congress. During this examination, bureau researchers must explain their requests, identify the need for an investigation in the area, and demonstrate why the applied project should be worth the investment. It is at this point that those making the request must rely heavily on pure research findings in order to justify progressing to the applied stage. This approval process results in a continuous link between pure and applied researchers within the organization. And it also produces a situation that makes it impossible for bureau researchers to forget which superiors they must please in order to move ahead with their work.

To secure information about the types of programs or research most likely needed, BOM researchers rely heavily on those within the organization who do market research. By keeping attuned in this way, bureau researchers increase the probability of their programs being defined as relevant by those who must approve them. These relationships provide another element of coordination within the bureau; and they are further cemented by the fact that the data collectors also come to rely heavily upon BOM scientists for information about technological developments that they use in their projections.

So, despite its highly decentralized research operations and its distinctively different services, BOM is an organization that is more directed toward common purposes than might be supposed. It has developed a long-standing, general mission to perform vis-à-vis private industry; and bureau researchers direct themselves toward practical problems and answers that either are or can be made evident to the various superiors who sanction their work. Neither "mad scientists" nor uncompromising dreamers can occupy much of a place in the modern bureaucratic world of the Bureau of Mines.

IMPLEMENTATION AND REGULATION

The bureau implements its research programs by disseminating information to potential users. If no one picks up and continues to apply the bureau's findings, its work is wasted. Several series of publications including information circulars, bulletins, technical progress reports, and reports of investigation, a newsletter called *Technology News*, pilot plants open for investigation, and sponsored seminars are all devices employed to bring BOM research to practitioners. In addition, BOM personnel publish in technical journals, write for trade magazines, attend conventions, and operate demonstration projects at industry trade shows to serve their audience. Even more directly, researchers will, if requested, work with technical users to apply BOM findings to new construction projects or reconversions. At times the bureau will even share costs on such cooperative ventures.

TABLE 2.1

TECHNOLOGY TRANSFER TO USER ORGANIZATIONS

Area of Technology	User
Mining and reclamation research	Mining companies; state and local governments, especially metal divisions
Coal combustion	Utility companies
Synthetic fuels; waste-to-oil conversion	Utility and petroleum companies; chemical process industry; gas industry; small industries requiring clean sources of power
Natural gas and petroleum simulation	Petroleum and gas companies
Oil shale	Petroleum and chemical companies
Urban refuse	State and local government; scrap processors
Junk cars	Scrap processors
Stack gas cleaning	Copper and lead smelters; power plants
Waste stabilization	Mining and ore beneficial operations
Industrial wastes	Iron and steel mills; nonferrous metal processors; aircraft and auto industry; metal finishers

Source: Federal Council for Science and Technology, Committee on Domestic Technology Transfer, *Directory of Federal Technology Transfer* (Washington, D.C.: U.S. Government Printing Office, 1975), p. 132.

Historically most technology transfer has been to the private sector. (See Table 2.1.) This has allowed industries such as mining companies and chemical processors to extract more, lower costs, develop better products from raw material, and make more retail goods available to the public. However, in recent years, BOM has provided assistance to a growing number of users. Unions like the United Mine Workers have used BOM reports on increasing mine safety to press demands for better working conditions in collective bargaining with mining companies. Other bureaus like the Environmental Protection Agency and the Mining Enforcement and Safety Administration request and receive assistance in setting regulatory standards for pollution levels and safety standards. And many state and local units of government come to the bureau for designs and specifications for utility operations, building standards, recycling projects, refuse containment, and answers to innumerable other public problems. Without a doubt, the increasing number of organizations facing technical problems related to metals, minerals, and fossil fuels is developing a new set of clients for BOM beyond the old-line industries.

BOM's emerging clientele has complicated the implementation of its programs immeasurably. The complexity results because of the bureau's unique advisory role relative to these various users. Unlike most other bureaus, BOM does not set regulations directly. If an industry or local government desires to duplicate one of the bureau's pilot plants, that user is free to adopt those innovations it finds appealing and leave those that appear inapplicable. BOM cannot force duplication of the entire effort unless a cost-sharing agreement is in effect, an infrequent situation.

As a result, when the Bureau of Mines desires to serve as a model for technological developments beyond its organizational structure, it must plan its pilot projects with implementation and technology transfer in mind. And it must develop various alternatives that potential users can select from prior to beginning their own construction. But the bureau can do this only by systematically examining a variety of external environmental conditions and including relevant modifications of pilot projects in its presentations and reports. Without determining how varying environmental aspects affect pilot operations, the bureau can never control for variations in site locations, transportation factors, or dozens of other factors affecting different users. Without knowledge about the specific client's setting, BOM cannot even serve as a particularly valuable information source or advisor. More and more, the bureau is doing all of these things.

To some extent, the bureau has moved in this direction in order to provide greater assistance. But its involvement as an advisor to other bureaus with important regulatory responsibilities is an even more important reason for the change. Within the Office of Energy and Minerals, the Mining Enforcement and Safety Administration regulates mine safety and inspects for violations; but the Bureau of Mines is authorized to perform research related to MESA's enforcement role. The existence of several similar arrangements involving other federal and state government bureaus allows BOM to be a most important advisor to those who need to conform to regulatory standards.

Although the bureau's regulatory recommendations are only advisory, its standards are applied and followed by regulators because they are legitimized by expert research and inquiry that would otherwise be lacking. In a word, the bureau has *status* with those who set the rules for related environmental, safety, and consumer issues. And that makes the bureau's efforts crucial to those in industry and government who construct projects applying its technology. These users realize that BOM pilot projects meet, indeed often determine, acceptable regulatory standards. And they understand that they, as operators, will be required to meet those standards. So users willingly rely on BOM advice; but they do so only when that organization's research meets their specific requirements. That fact makes it crucial for the bureau's research to be technically exacting and still applicable to many settings if BOM programs are to be effectively implemented.

SUCCESS AND FAILURE

The question of successes and failures in programs depends on the perspective of whoever makes the judgment. From the bureau's perspective, it could be claimed that any research effort that gets funded at the applied level is a success, and any research that fails to produce a funded program is unsuccessful. If that is the criterion, success means gaining additional income to keep employment and productivity within the bureau constant or growing. And it would indicate that 1972 was one of the bureau's most successful years within the past decade since BOM received a substantial increase over 1971 funds for conservation and development of mineral resources, $500,000 for research on geothermal resources and sulfur utilization, $800,000 for research on filling critical mine void areas, and $300,000 for planning and designing a pilot plant to convert wood wastes to low-sulfur oil.

For the Bureau of Mines, however, the number of new programs per year is not necessarily the best indicator of its success. Pure research produces programs but it is often aimed at modification of ongoing ones. And, under other circumstances, pure research that is judged competent, thorough, and rewarding to BOM often indicates that a new program is not needed. For these reasons, two other indicators of success appear to be better measures: direct transfer of technology to users and continuation of programs in a given area. Both of these suggest that the bureau's research efforts are either producing or on the verge of producing societal benefits.

The first indicator, technology transfer, provides a great deal of evidence about the success of BOM. The massive coal shale strip mines and large-scale sale of oil shale rights in public lands in Wyoming and Montana have been encouraged by bureau research into the feasibility of producing usable products from low grade shale. Strip mine reclamation, especially in the South and Midwest, is an even better example, since the reclamation process involving fly ash was developed entirely by BOM researchers. Likewise, it was bureau research that led to industrial usage of previously unusable low grade nonmagnetic taconite. In this case, the Michigan iron range became a productive area because BOM discovered how to upgrade worthless taconite to produce pellets for fueling blast furnaces. The bureau has successfully transferred an even greater variety of smaller scale devices and techniques. These include a technique for sealing off underground gas fires by remote operations, another for lowering the noise level of pneumatic drill equipment, rock bolts in mines for increased structural soundness, and mine communication hardware. In terms of actual productivity, the bureau developed leaching techniques presently accounting for industry's ability to recover 6 percent of the annual production of gold in the United States. Previously this metal would have been nonrecoverable in the production process.

The second indicator, continued program research, suggests great promise of potential benefits. BOM's metallurgy division believes it is on the verge of breakthroughs in the recovery of aluminum, copper, and silver. And research in the conversion of refuse and waste to fuel is continuing even after some applications have been successfully operated by bureau clients.

Failures have been notable as well, however. For every technique or device that has worked, an untold number failed. Black lung disease, most notably, continues to be a seemingly insurmountable health hazard in coal mining. Some programs simply have been unworkable; and limits in research capabilities prevented others from producing results.

The bureau has experienced other kinds of failures as well though. Many workable programs that pose no insurmountable research obstacles have perplexed bureau officials. A compensation program for miners and widows of miners victimized by black lung disease proved difficult to implement; and the bureau was criticized for its inability to identify eligible parties, investigate claims, and deliver compensation. In fairness to BOM, however, this was a program unique, even alien, to its operations. The same was true for programs that authorized BOM to regulate and investigate safety operations in industrial areas under its jurisdiction. However, the bureau faced additional charges of failing to support its on-site investigators and not getting tough with industry in the implementation of safety programs. As a result of alleged inadequacies, the Bureau of Mines has lost programs. The Mining Enforcement and Safety Administration was created in 1973 to take over BOM's compensation and regulatory responsibilities and undertake related activities in safety, enforcement, education, training, and the assessment of penalties for violators.[5] BOM has suffered similar criticism since 1973, primarily for leaving the development of energy policies to private industry, and has seen much of its fuel-related research transferred to the Federal Energy Administration and Energy Research and Development Administration.

Much of the criticism of the Bureau of Mines in the mid-1970's has been overly harsh and inspired by position-taking politicians wanting the public spotlight. However, it has been clear that BOM has been unable to satisfy the recipients of programs not falling into its normal research-oriented system of operations. Claims that BOM is a captive of industry are grossly exaggerated; but the observation that the bureau cannot provide services independently of its industrial partners appears to be an accurate one. Even in its indirect regulatory role, the organization advises with its long-time clients in mind. Although BOM recommendations to, for instance, the Environmental Protection Agency are pains-takingly researched with environmental conditions foremost in mind, bureau researchers are constantly aware that the big part of their job will come later in helping industrial technology users adapt to whatever regulations result.

ITS VALUE TO OTHERS

The working bureaucrats of the Bureau of Mines include trained engineers, metallurgists, plant managers, and economists. As a group, they are one of the best-trained and most specialized bureaus in government. The nature of their work makes their skills a necessity. And a combination of personal skills and type of work makes BOM one of the most potentially valuable bureaus imaginable.

The bureau's value to the national interest is unmistakable. Energy and raw materials are resources basic to the continued economic viability of the United States. But there is more of value within BOM than benefits distributed collectively to the whole society. As already noted, various clients selectively receive assistance from the bureau. To these clients in industry and government, BOM is an organizational resource. It saves them time and a great deal of manpower, and it does so at little or no financial cost.

Petroleum, coal, and metal producers have, in the past at least, gained the most from the bureau.[6] Presently, that condition may be slowly changing, with other bureaus and local governments making increased use of BOM. However, working relationships that have developed over the past few decades give individual firms and their trade associations in the big three industries more access to and a greater working knowledge of the bureau than any other client. Although no clients get all they want from BOM, there is little or nothing of concern within the organization that is not quickly communicated to such private interest groups as the American Mining Congress, the National Coal Association, and the Petroleum Association of America. In fact, staff members from these organizations are regularly and voluntarily contacted by BOM's division officials to seek advice on the appropriateness of possible new programs. Yet no such deference is accorded the representative of American municipalities, the National League of Cities.

Several things about BOM are important for industry and cause its representatives to intervene in bureau operations. First of all, industrial clients want BOM's continued support, since it amounts to a subsidy for their own operations. But, to have the bureau work effectively for them, their clients need input for recommending research goals. A second factor of importance is keeping BOM away from research that is potentially profitable to private business. Industries must maintain their own experts for extraction and production, and these personnel can oftentimes develop money-making and patentable devices and techniques while doing this work. Therefore, industry representatives want to keep BOM informed as to what research areas to ignore so government doesn't duplicate private efforts. Finally, industry wants to guide BOM toward continuing research in areas where there is already a large private investment. Industrial clients do not want the bureau developing alternative natural resources that would undermine present operations and sunk costs. The oil industry is the best example of success with regard to this concern. In the 1950's, primarily at oil producers' urging, the bureau's original pilot plant for converting gas to oil was closed and sold to a private company for approximately one-seventh of the project's total previous research costs.[7]

Elected politicians, especially in the Congress, also find the bureau a personally valuable political resource. There are subcommittees in both the House of Representatives and the Senate that supervise bureau programs and both are dominated by legislators whose districts and states contain industries affected by BOM.[8] The Senate subcommittee on Minerals, Materials, and Fuels has nine members, and at least seven of them represented such states in 1976. In the House, the Mines and Mining subcommittee has nineteen members, and all but two had constituencies with an interest in the bureau. For electoral reasons, most subcommittee members have some reason to want to be able to influence the Bureau of Mines. And, with regard to their ability to effectively sway fellow members in the Congress toward support of "back home" programs, these same subcommittee members want direct access to BOM information that can aid them. To these individuals, the bureau provides more than an assist. They literally use the bureau to survive in their careers.

The President, in contrast, has little interest in what the Bureau of Mines does because its work is of little value to national politics. This is especially true since energy research, and much of the bureau's resulting political visibility, was taken away. Given presidential priorities, this situation does not seem likely to change in the 1980's; and, as a result, congressional subcommittee members will exercise a greater voice than the President in determining what programs the bureau will undertake. These legislators and private industries presently find the bureau to be of greatest value. Consequently, they are the ones who work hardest to control it.

SUMMARY

No two bureaus are exactly alike, either in structure or operation. It could be no other way, since bureaus are organized according to their own unique mission and programs. The Bureau of Mines, except for its limited regulatory authority, is not unlike most other bureaus at any level of government. It engages in the same type of activity, and its political concerns are similar. Therefore, this chapter should, in general, familiarize readers with what a bureau is and what it does.

BOM lacks political visibility. It is neither recognizable to large numbers of Americans, nor does its hierarchical position within the Department of Interior make it an easily identifiable part of the bureaucratic maze. As a part of DOI, the Bureau of Mines is only one of the crowd. Yet the bureau performs important research services for society if one considers the immense number of needs met by the mining industry. BOM has incredibly broad responsibilities for minerals, metals, and energy sources as mine products. Accordingly, the bureau has developed an extensive clientele among those who will profit most from its research and development work: the mining industrialists.

Two things become apparent if one reflects carefully on BOM's operation: the importance of government's technological involvement and the reason why so few people become aware of it. Quite simply, bureaus like BOM directly service only a small segment of society. The rest of us certainly benefit from these services, but do so very indirectly. In fact, most individuals know very little or nothing about how minerals, metals, and energy sources are made into usable products. So it is hardly surprising that these same people ignore the existence and operation of service bureaus like this one.

The rest of this book examines the place of bureaus in American politics. How important are they? How extensive is their political influence and involvement? What kind of a leadership role do they play in setting political priorities? How do they assume such leadership? What do they get from their political involvement? How do they get what they want? These are the questions addressed in subsequent chapters.

The second section, Chapters 3 and 4, examines the political environment of bureaus and the specifics of their relationship to other political institutions. This section is intended to be a general description of bureau relationships; while admittedly simplified, the chapters are designed to show what political pressures influence the development of public programs. Then, in Section III, the book turns to the actual work of bureaus. Chapter 5 is about program development within bureaus and their corresponding problems. Chapter 6 looks at bureaus and their various concerns as programs are implemented and evaluated. Chapter 7 is an examination of the regulatory powers of the bureaus. Finally, Chapters 8 and 9 draw some conclusions about the place of the public bureaucracy in American politics and the unlikely prospects for bureaucratic change.

SECTION TWO

THE POLITICAL ENVIRONMENT
OF BUREAUCRACY

3...

POLITICAL INSTITUTIONS
and the BUREAU

Governmental programs, at the national level, are most often given the imprimatur of the President holding office at the time of their proposal. And, increasingly over the past century, it has become the President, rather than a congressman, who utters the first public words on programmatic needs. This identification has created a popular image that twists President Harry Truman's famous quotation, "the buck stops here." Today it almost seems as if that governmental "buck" revolves exclusively around the President; that, indeed, he personifies government.

This was clearly the case during Lyndon Johnson's presidency. His domestic goals came to be collectively defined as the "Great Society," and the resulting social programs were identified in the press and on television as Johnson's creations. President Johnson also served during the war in Vietnam, and his orders directly led to escalation of the war and to historically unparalleled air raids. The war too was laid at his feet. For his presence at the top, Lyndon Johnson was praised as a saint and damned as a fool, depending on what decision his critics were looking at and what beliefs they held. Johnson was adulated and criticized as a leader on the basis of the successes and failures of specific programs, be they bombings or urban training centers. Such are the yardsticks by which he and all other Presidents have come to be measured.

The attention recently focused on Henry Kissinger has provided the general public more information about the reality of political decision-making, however. People no longer see just the President at work. It has become obvious that Kissinger, in addition to Presidents Nixon and Ford, played a critical role in deciding what actions to take in foreign affairs. His accepted expertise, and the resulting dependency of elected

45

leaders on him, reveals that the President is limited and constrained by what help others can provide. Kissinger, as both presidential advisor and Secretary of State, exhibits the resources and strengths of the bureaucrat.

David Halberstam, in his best-selling account of the war in Vietnam, demonstrates the same point.[1] The leadership that arrived at crucial decisions was a collective one. John F. Kennedy and Lyndon Johnson never acted alone. These Presidents listened to many varying arguments, and then made their own choices. At their least, these men were won over by whichever advisors made the strongest arguments and possessed the greatest control over the President. In some instances, Kennedy and Johnson were both clearly without any real freedom of choice due to the manner in which decisions were presented to them by advisors. All any President can claim, in truth, is final responsibility, not final or absolute discretion to do whatever he wishes. Too often this point is overlooked, even by the occupant of that office. Again, Lyndon Johnson provides an excellent illustration. Once, on hearing that "his" helicopter had arrived, President Johnson turned to a young soldier and remarked "Son, they're all my helicopters." But only the public, and perhaps an overly egotistical President, ever believed that this man was able to do just as he wished with all the personnel and equipment theoretically at his command.

This dependency goes far beyond the confines of the White House and the President's personal advisors. All of these individuals merely sort through previously compiled information. Only on the most important decisions, or in an extreme crisis, do they react first-hand to newly generated information such as air photos or communiqués from foreign powers. The rest of the time, even on matters of great importance, the Henry Kissingers and Robert McNamaras rely on information and recommendations supplied by bureaus or fact-finding agencies such as the Office of Management and Budget. As a result, the successes and failures of their decisions are likely to rest on the reliability and thoroughness of bureau reports. For instance, President Kennedy, during the Cuban missile crisis, found himself operating on the mistaken assumption that U.S. offensive missiles had been previously removed from Turkey at his insistence.[2] It was only when Russia demanded the removal of these very missiles that Kennedy found they were still there. State and Defense Department officials had refused to comply with his earlier orders because they contended that this action would jeopardize U.S.-Turkish relations and the programs they had designed to sustain them.

Examples like this are not uncommon in American politics. At another point during the Cuban crisis, Kennedy was similarly misinformed about air strike capabilities. He requested data about the potential success of surgical air strikes against missile sites on the island and, instead, without being told the difference, was supplied with information on the likelihood of success for a full-scale attack.[3] This projection had been the only one determined by the Air Force and, as a result, was the only programmatic response made available for the President and his advisors when they chose between air intervention and the alternative of a naval blockade.

The day-to-day decisions of government rely, even more exclusively, on bureau reports. Neither a President nor his advisors can spend time proposing solutions for society's infinite problems. As Richard Nixon once observed: "I've always thought this country could run itself domestically . . . You need a President for a foreign policy."[4] To govern everything, the chief executive would need to surround himself with individual advisors on inland waterways, housing, mass transit, environmental impact, and innumerable other problem areas. The White House, under such conditions, would be bulging at the seams due to this influx of advisors; and, more importantly, the President would fail to establish the necessary trust and rapport which can be gained only through regular and continuous personal interaction. Dozens of individual advisors would come to be no more than a faceless crowd with doubtful value to the President. The necessary loyalty, and probably the necessary information, can be obtained directly from bureau specialists who need not be paid to sit around, full-time, at the White House.

It must be realized that presidential decisions are not just the product of one man's efforts, nor even of those of a few people at the pinnacle of national power. Decisions or directives that are announced from the White House, or for that matter from a governor's or mayor's mansion, result from collective efforts at the top and bottom. Bureau officials generate data and plan responses, and then inform the chief executive of what they've found. The amount of discretion the executive has varies with the strength of the report and the depth of his own personal convictions. But, under any circumstances, it takes an extremely secure leader to deviate very far from the recommendations of experts.

No President can spend enough time on routine, noncrisis affairs to feel safe in his convictions when the bureaucracy disagrees. An executive, at times, may have a pet issue or be ideologically at odds with bureaucratic proposals. Then the man at the top dominates even the most routine decision. Lyndon Johnson, for instance, concocted and promoted a plan for a Head Start school program, and the Office of Economic Opportunity gave it priority status because of his insistence. However, most of the time, it is only natural for the President to assume that the responsible bureau is presenting the best plan possible. And, after that, the President has few other options than to use his personal advisors and his own intuition to carefully check the rationale and logic of the plan's proponents.

EXECUTIVE LEADERSHIP

The popular image of the President as primary facilitator and proponent of public programs comes from the constitutional model of United States government as it has evolved. Constitutionally, the President is the leader, and the Congress investigates and debates the applicability of his programs. In this model, the chief executive proposes solutions to public problems, and the legislature disposes of his proposal. There are, however, in practice, endless variations upon the interaction between these two branches of government. The above situation is only a simplified version of the norm, or general turn of events. "Separation of powers" and the attendant "checks and balances" do not lock the Congress into an advisory role. In fact, congressmen and legislators in all American governments are free to offer their own programs for direct legislative action. And they regularly do.

The norm prevails, though, and not without reason. The President, quite simply, has many well-documented leadership advantages over Congress.[5] He is, for example, more able to react quickly to a crisis. Congress must go through the time-consuming task of calling a whole body of individuals together, and then the assembly must work a compromise. Also, the President, and not the Congress, is empowered to negotiate with representatives of foreign governments. Additional advantages could be listed that suggest this same feature of strength through solitary responsibility and the President's ability to act on his own. But to a great extent, such a list would be misleading because the advantages are little more than an elaboration on the executive's greatest strength vis-à-vis the legislature—his authority as chief administrator of the bureaucracy.

Bureaus are normally part of the *executive branch of government*, and the chief executive sits as its head. This, as has been discussed, means the President need not act alone. He has legitimate authority to direct the resources of the bureaucracy, but the Congress can make no such claim. In other words, much of the President's individual influence comes from his collective ties, not just his ability to act alone. Because of these ties, he is closer to information sources and more prone to be aware of new events than the typical legislator. Thus, in terms of presidential-congressional relations, it is the President who is more capable of proposing programs if he can actually make use of bureau resources.

An example of executive power based on bureaucratic capabilities and resources was one of the first major programs successfully proposed by President Jimmy Carter. After several new proposals and recommended changes from the White House had bogged down in other program areas, Carter found the Department of Housing and Urban Development responding quickly to his call for large increases in public housing assistance because he proposed to use the organization to *his* and *its* own advantage. HUD won such a large increase in its funding that the number of new public housing unit starts increased by nearly 600 percent, from 58,371 in budget year 1976 to approximately 334,000 in 1977. In addition, HUD bureaus responded to Carter initiatives by reviewing programs for mortgage interest subsidies and additional subsidies for the working poor, both previously ongoing programs but inoperative when Carter took office.

Using bureau resources is no easy matter, however. The skill and expertise of the bureaucrats are their own possessions, not the President's. Bureau officials do not engage in planning and research with the President or his personal advisors as active participants. Normally, the White House contributes ideas for program development. Bureau officials are told, as they were by President Carter, to develop "more extensive public housing programs" or, more specifically, "provide dramatic increases in the construction of federally subsidized housing units." Or, in another area of national need, military bureaucrats might be asked to provide a "defense plan using an optimal, but balanced, mix of nuclear and tactical weapons." The bureau's task is to take these directives and decide what is feasible. White House officials, for the most part, define guidelines for bureau officials in order to inform them of their discretionary limits. Bureaucrats learn that it will do little good to propose cutbacks in public housing for the poor or a defense system based exclusively on nuclear arms. The directives indicate that the President will reject such ideas outright.

Indeed rejection of bureau proposals is the real power of the chief executive in dealing with bureaus. The President or a governor can always refuse to accept and advocate the proposed program to the legislature. Oftentimes this threat will kill the matter entirely; and, if the bureau looks for legislative support, it must face the threat of a veto should the program ever be passed. For this reason, bureau officials take the directives of their executive quite seriously.

The ability to direct is no guarantee of executive leadership, however. President Ford, in the sharpest of words, spoke against a large gasoline tax in 1974 and early 1975, but various bureau officials in the Environmental Protection Agency and Department of the Treasury continued to promote such a plan anyway. They did so because these bureaucrats knew support existed among the President's own advisors and in Congress. Their own research efforts committed them to the idea, and the supportive words of these other allies made opposition to the President seem worthwhile. This kind of circumvention of executive directives is not only possible, it is likely and frequent when bureaucrats feel the cross-pressures of counterdirectives. The chief executive may be the chief administrator, but he is far from being the only politician with enough resources to affect bureau operations.

LEGISLATIVE POLITICS

Congressmen do not have formal administrative responsibility. Nonetheless, legislators like Representative Jamie Whitten have often been given such informal titles as "permanent Secretary of Agriculture."[6] This Mississippi Democrat's impact on the development of agricultural programs has undoubtedly been more substantial than that of any President. For over twenty years, Whitten prevented the Agriculture Department from undertaking any studies of the effects of agricultural change on people. His views led to a departmental emphasis on the problems of farms and crop production. Any other proposals were eliminated. As early as the mid-1940's, Whitten's influence was strong enough to kill research on the social and economic problems of black soldiers returning to the rural South. And, in the late 1960's, he was still able to have a study of malnutrition in Mississippi stopped. The important thing to realize is that Jamie Whitten's influence is not exceptional in Congress. Legislators do control bureau programs, at least sometimes.

Bureaus respond to legislative directives like Whitten's for two reasons: money and program approval. As previously noted, legislators can propose enabling acts as well as the chief executive. But, regardless of who proposes a program, the legislative body must pass the measure before it can be put into operation. In addition, the program must be funded, and this occurs as a legislative act separate from its approval. Thus, in order to get programs and funding, bureaus must please those legislators who can assist them.

The strength of individual legislators comes from the decentralized organizational structure of the legislature. Most of the work, probably 90 percent or more, goes on in the committees. Things are usually decided well in advance of floor action by the House or Senate as a whole, and the same is true of state legislatures and the legislative bodies in most of the large local governments (usually called commissions or boards). It is rare indeed that the outcome of a decision establishing a new program or continuing an old one is in doubt after committees have acted. The same is true about decisions on funding—that is, *appropriations*.

Committee systems are based on the need for *specialization* and a *division of labor* within the legislature, the same needs that led to the proliferation of bureaus. (See Illus. 3.1). The Congress of the United States, for example, faces over twenty thousand pieces of legislation a year.

ILLUSTRATION 3.1

AN EXAMPLE OF SUPPORT FOR THE COMMITTEE SYSTEM

THE FOLLOWING ARE LETTERS AND A TELEGRAM EXCERPTED FROM THE FILES OF
REPRESENTATIVE RICHARD BOLLING (D. MO.). BOLLING, THE MAJOR CONGRESSIONAL
ADVOCATE OF LEGISLATIVE REFORM, CHAIRED A SELECT COMMITTEE ON COMMITTEES
TO REDESIGN THE HOUSE COMMITTEE SYSTEM. THAT SPECIAL COMMITTEE ISSUED ITS
REPORT, WENT OUT OF EXISTENCE, AND HAD ALMOST NONE OF ITS PROPOSED RE-
FORMS INACTED. WHY WAS THIS SPECIALIST IGNORED ? BECAUSE HE WANTED TO
DISRUPT THE ENVIRONMENT IN WHICH "WHIRLPOOLS"OPERATE. THATS WHY.

My dear Colleague Dick:
    I called at your office today to
personally extend my congratulations
on your splendid performance as
Chairman of the Committee of the
Whole during the lengthy debate on
the energy crisis bill. You pre-
sided with great skill and ability
and deserve the applause of your
Colleagues.
    As the author of noted books on
Congress--I think immediately of
your book House Out of Order--I know
that you are an authority on the
Congress and would make an able
Speaker.
    I wanted to ask you what I can do
to cause you as Chairman of the
Select Committee on Small Business...
    With kindest regards and best
wishes to you and yours for the
Holiday Season, I am
Sincerely your friend,
Joe L. Evins, M.C.
Fourth Dist., Tenn.
Chairman, Small Business Committee

THE PROPELLER CLUB, PORT OF NEW OR-
LEANS CHAPTER LARGEST IN THE WORLD
WITH 850 MEMBERS, ACTIVELY ENGAGED IN
MARITIME AFFAIRS IN THIS THE 3RD
LARGEST PORT OF THE WORLD, STRONGLY
SUPPORTS THE CONTINUATION OF THE
MERCHANT MARINE AND FISHERIES COM-
MITTEE...

Dear Dick:
    The Select Committee on Committees
of which you are Chairman has proposed
an excellent plan for reorganization
of the House to meet the problems facing
us today. However, one item of that
proposal is of deep concern to me.
That is the removal of legislative
jurisdiction over the Tennessee Valley
Authority from the Public Works Committee....
Sincerely yours,
Robert E. Jones
Fifth Dist., Ala.
Member, Committee on Public Works

UNIONS REPRESENTING MORE THAN 1 MILL-
ION FEDERAL AND POSTAL WORKERS DEEPLY
CONCERNED ABOUT FUTURE OF HOUSE POST
OFFICE AND CIVIL SERVICE COMMITTEE AND
OTHER COMMITTEES...

Dear Dick:
    The Division of Vocational and Tech-
nical Education of the Mississippi
State Department of Education has
recently contacted me about your proposal to place Vocational Education
and Manpower under the proposed Committee on Labor of the House. They
are bitterly and vociferously opposed
to it.
Sincerely,
David R. Bowen
Second Dist., Miss.

SOURCE: HARPER'S WEEKLY 64 (JANUARY 17, 1975), P. 16

Of course only a small percentage of them are seriously considered, but the average congressman could never become even minimally informed about each of the remaining two thousand or more bills that advance. In order to make the necessary decisions, most legislators come to rely on a variety of sources for cues as to the meaning of the proposals. Their own staffs, political parties, house leaders, legislative friends, constituents, interest groups, the media, and many others are of personal value in helping decide. But the contact with and concern of these sources both are like the weather, intermittent and variable. They aren't always watching everything. Accordingly, their assistance to the individual legislator varies as well.

As a result, committees have emerged as the one source of political direction which can always be counted on.[7] All bills go to the committees for action in each legislative house; and, in the committees, interested specialists make the recommendations they see fit. The committee systems in most legislatures are quite well developed in terms of coverage of most problem areas and legislator membership. There is normally an already established standing committee *with jurisdiction* over types of proposals, and this provides an important routine for house deliberations. The House Appropriations Committee, for example, is always ready to receive proposals for the yearly appropriations bill and will occasionally authorize special appropriations as well. Similarly, the House Agriculture Committee would be the one to act on any new proposals to approve programs for agricultural production; and the Armed Services Committee would do the same for any defense construction programs. Only under the most extreme conditions, and only if the legislative leadership can come up with a good rationale, are these committees ever circumvented. But, even if one committee is avoided, another must be given a chance to handle the bill prior to house passage.

The committee system is even more finely specialized than this at the national level and in most state governments. This is accomplished through proliferation of *subcommittees* which have jurisdiction over more clearly defined problem areas within the committee's overall assignment. For instance, the House Agriculture Committee is subdivided into units dealing with cotton commodities, forests, domestic marketing, rural development, and six other areas. The Senate Labor and Public Welfare Committee has twelve subcommittees specializing in such things as aging, health, and human resources. In all, the thirty-eight committees of the U.S. House and Senate have a total of more than three hundred subcommittees, and a large and active state legislature may have nearly as many.

The involvement of all members is as important to the operation of the committee system as the routine nature of program jurisdiction.

Everyone is involved; and, as long as the individual is willing "to do his homework" and demonstrates expertise in the assigned area, everyone can become a respected legislator to whom others listen. *Reciprocity* and *mutual trust* are the unwritten rules which hold the committee system together. Legislators usually have more than one committee assignment, but it is rare to find someone actually becoming very active in more than one of them. Instead, successful legislators usually work to become especially knowledgeable about the jurisdictional problems of one assignment, and then they try to become opinion leaders for their colleagues throughout the legislature on those issues.

In other words, dependency develops. The workload of the legislature is immense; so individuals divide up the work and assume the responsibility for one type of problem. And, as long as they demonstrate their competency, others listen to them. This is how legislation gets passed, how the work gets done. Of course, partisan, ideological, and other differences still matter; but not to the extent that they permanently match legislators against one another. The important point is that legislators do become resident experts within their own houses and are deferred to as such. Therefore, these other differences matter much less than might otherwise be expected because the committee system is the major organizational feature of the legislature.

This is why legislators like Jamie Whitten can have such a substantial effect on the programs developed by a bureau. Whitten has for more than twenty years held "the power of the purse" over the Agriculture Department by serving as Chairman of the subcommittee on agriculture of the House Appropriations Committee. If Representative Whitten is irritated, funds can be lost. And if funds are lost, so are programs and, eventually, bureaucratic jobs. Whitten's influence, however, does not just derive from his chairmanship. His knowledge of agricultural affairs and his colleagues' reactions are his principal resources. He has been described as a conscientious student of every line of the agriculture budget, "a man whose hawkeye is legendary among department officials."[8] Jamie Whitten directs because congressmen, on and off the committee, understand his prowess. They know that Whitten fully understands his legislative job. Perhaps, also, as a detractor says of his relationship with others, he has a "wily ability to juggle figures and cloud ideas."[9] Nevertheless, when Whitten cuts a program from Agriculture, it stays cut. Chairmen can be overruled and floor amendments made, but legislative leaders like Whitten persist through their own abilities. And so bureaus pay heed.

The legislator who tries to work hard and gain the respect of his colleagues faces a difficult task. To a great extent, the work he does must be his own; and, he must meet other obligations, such as getting reelected, at the same time. Legislators lack the luxury of the chief executive's staff. The Congress of the United States employs approximately 32,790 staff members to assist over 535 legislators, but this includes clerks, typists, and other nonprofessionals. The President, by way of contrast, had a White House staff of nearly five hundred in 1974. State legislators are much worse off, usually relying on a secretary and the small staff of a legislative research bureau of some kind. Even that, however, is more than most local government legislators have. Usually, except in the largest and most progressive cities and counties, they possess nothing other than their own ingenuity. So, if a legislator is to gain a position of prominence in dealing with bureaus, it must be done with a good deal of effort and perseverance over a period of time.

Of course, time is not something most legislators have in abundance. They have many tasks to perform; and, although some hold office and committee assignments for twenty years or more, many others have only a short tenure. This, again, is especially true at the state and local level. As a result, legislators are forced to look beyond their own immediate experiences for answers to their questions, especially to interest groups and even bureaus themselves. Oftentimes, in fact, these are the only sources for information and data about program needs. This, however, presents a special danger because the legislator can, unwittingly perhaps, become a puppet of those sources. Nothing the legislator does will lose his colleagues' respect any quicker. As a result, a legislator like Barry Goldwater must do a balancing act. He relies on the materials from the Air Force as his primary source of data about programmatic needs for his special area of expertise, tactical air power. But he subjects this material to as much personal scrutiny as possible in order to look for discrepancies, and he also goes to as many other sources of information as he possibly can to cross-check.

The difficulty and personal costs of such an assignment very easily explain why many legislators are never able to influence bureau decisions in any significant way. An astute political observer summed this deficiency up very neatly by saying "If you're gonna play, ya gotta pay." Or as Goldwater himself once claimed, "there is no such thing as a free lunch." Hard work is the stuff of politics when legislators desire to direct the bureaucracy.

INTEREST GROUPS

Interest groups, because they are not formal governmental institutions with legal powers, lack the direct control of bureaus that a chief executive or legislator can have. But, despite the fact that their consent is not formally needed before programs are enacted and funded, interest groups still have important resources at their disposal. And they often get their way on matters of program development and implementation.

Interest groups largely derive their strength from their ability to provide valuable information to government decision-makers.[10] In this sense, they are much like bureaus. Most of them are highly organized with staffs that do research and become expert in matters relating to the group's governmental involvement. But, rather than determining program needs, they usually attempt to measure the likely effect of already proposed programs on their members. Legislators, as noted earlier, find interest groups quite helpful in overcoming their reliance on bureaucratically supplied material. Therefore, they tend to look for and actively seek out interest group contact. Interestingly enough, the same is true of bureau officials themselves. Some data about programmatic needs can more easily be obtained by going to one of these organizations than by gathering it directly. For instance, the National Association of Housing and Redevelopment Officials (NAHRO) has accumulated vast reservoirs of information about low-cost housing, and it would hardly make sense for Community Development and Planning personnel to ignore it when doing research in that area. It is generally more efficient to go to an interest group for any desired information that its members might have or that could easily be collected from them.

The willingness of interest groups to supply information to government officials should not be surprising. After all, this provides them an opportunity to have a bureau consider their observations early in the process of deliberations about program needs. The ability to communicate with bureau officials and supply them with information supportive of the group's position certainly provides an advantage when it comes to obtaining the goals these groups want through government programs. As a lobbyist for one of the urban interest groups once said: "Lobbying, to me, is just sitting down with people and telling them how I see it. That's how I get what I want."[11]

Bureaus and interest groups, to a great extent, need one another. The bureaus occupy a key political position in program development that cannot be ignored, and the groups supply information that facilitates their work. In addition, they have a mutual need because the two are potentially in conflict with one another; and this conflict is damaging to both. Bureau officials, in particular, find their situation precarious because they must decide whether or not to accept an interest group's position. If they reject the group's claims, they must expect its staff to oppose bureau recommendations elsewhere. Group representatives will go on to lobby executives, committee specialists, their staff, and other legislators as a last resort to gain desired changes. Public relations campaigns, constituent pressure, electoral threats, and other tactics may be used to convince these politicians to oppose bureau recommendations. All of this activity undermines confidence in the bureau's information.

Thus, the potential for conflict causes bureau personnel to listen to interest groups with special care. They are not merely providing information; they are also threatening to make the bureau's work more difficult by providing political obstacles that may undermine its efforts. Thus, straightforward opposition to an interest group is often avoided even though bureau officials fail to entirely agree with its staff. As a result, the two sides frequently attempt to strike an acceptable compromise to mute future opposition to the program.

Compromises are most likely to occur between bureaus and interest groups which interact regularly. Not even the Executive Director of the National Association of Manufacturers would expect too much attention were he to appear in the headquarters of the National Park Service to oppose a program on reforestation in national parks. His organization might not even be known, and even if it were, its political clout would not be viewed as too strong in relationship to park programs. The association lacks a history of involvement in that area, it lacks information and research to assist park officials, and it lacks the attention of other politicians concerned about park problems. The opposition of that group would undoubtedly create a furor in any one of several bureaus of the U.S. Department of Commerce, however. NAM lobbyists carefully scrutinize all Commerce programs for their effect on American business, and they regularly seek to assist Commerce in the development of their programs. In addition, NAM lobbyists know all of the pertinent people to turn to should they ever receive a cold shoulder from the bureaucrats.

Students of public administration have paid a great deal of attention to groups which regularly support or oppose a particular bureau's programs. They have labeled them the bureau's *clientele*.[12]

Clientele groups, by definition, are listened to on a regular basis. They are routinely sought out by bureau officials, and bureau doors are always open to them. Also, because it is their opposition which can be least afforded, clientele groups are the most likely to be able to bargain successfully with the bureau over program changes. Bureau personnel will work hard to see that changes are made to insure their support. In other words, bureaus establish a close working relationship with their clients, and this relationship thrusts these groups into political prominence.

Obviously, this gives some interest groups the ability to direct, at least in part, the content of government programs; and it leaves most others outside of the decisional process. All interest groups will not have this directive ability or share it equally. In order to become a valued client, a group must first have a bureau and programs to which to attach itself. The United States, for example, has only recently instituted the Consumer Protection Agency and given it some authority over consumer programs. Prior to its establishment, a consumer-oriented interest group would have been almost totally without a place to be heard. Additionally, however, the bureau must listen to the group if the group is to be powerful. And, bureaus will pay heed to the groups that can provide the best assistance or the most political opposition. Therefore, groups with bigger budgets, more members, a more skilled staff, greater prestige and the like have an advantage with a bureau.

But, even this advantage will not make an interest group very influential if the government as a whole rejects the recommendations of the bureau. If, for example, the Congress refuses to pass any consumer protection programs, it would be impossible to claim that consumer interest groups are important even though the Consumer Protection Agency accepts all of their recommendations. Political resources are cumulative, and their effect on government programs can be understood only by examining the combined resources of various political forces and observing how they interact. It is insufficient to look at just the chief executive, the legislature, or interest groups by themselves as has been done so far.

WHIRLPOOLS OF ACTIVITY

Politicians may, in the case of a given program, deal with any number of people in order to bargain for what they want incorporated into the proposal. It is possible to think of almost anyone in a particular political setting talking with any other participant to gain the desired results. The following scenario is an illustration of what could happen.

Congressman A, over his morning coffee, notes an item in a *Washington Post* column quoting informed, but unnamed, Interior Department sources about a plan under consideration to allow restricted strip mining on federally owned lands. We might imagine our aroused legislator jumping up and calling an immediate strategy meeting of his staff because of his opposition to the idea. Then we can envision phone calls of protest to the

White House, Secretary of Interior, Environmental Protection Agency, majority and minority House leaders, and Democratic party officials. At the same time, his staff could be calling together members of the Democratic Study Group and representatives of such liberal interest groups as the Sierra Club and Americans for Democratic Action. Finally, we can imagine a noon press conference being called where Congressman A announces his opposition and informs the media and public of the grave problem at hand.

How realistic is this scenario? Similar activity did happen, after all, in response to political announcements made during the Vietnam war, the Watergate affair, and the economic-energy crisis. At least, press reports led people to believe that angry legislators responded with such fury on these occasions. The illustration presented above, however, is completely unrealistic and would almost certainly never happen unless some strange additive were put into Congressman A's morning coffee. A plan to consider strip mining is a routine bureau activity. In its early stages, it would not merit the frantic attention reserved for events that rock the entire political system.

In the first place, such a response would be wasted energy. Those being called would be unable to take direct action against a plan that has not yet been presented. Party officials and the house leadership, in particular, have next to no control over programs like this one, especially during early planning.

The action could be counterproductive as well. Congressman A might gain by having bureau planners scrap the proposal in order to avoid a confrontation. But, on the other hand, bureau planners might also use the opportunity to mobilize support among administrators, legislators, and interest group representatives who have concern for protecting the bureau from outside meddling. At the extreme, they might force the early support of politicians who would otherwise take a hard and careful look at such a program during its preparatory period. The aroused congressman, no matter what the outcome, would end up looking like an hysterical neophyte; and he would probably make dangerous political enemies by antagonizing and embarrassing others with such an outrageous production.

In reality, politicians do not go around talking to everybody who could possibly become involved in a political decision. Only in a real crisis, or as a last resort on a matter of extreme personal importance, does a politician "pull out all the plugs." A much more likely scenario would proceeed in the following manner after Congresswoman B reads the same item and becomes similarly irritated.

First, she finishes the coffee and the paper. Then she goes to the office as usual and looks over her mail. While doing so, she requests a staff member to find out who would be most knowledgeable and informed about the strip mining matter, probably someone on either the House or the Senate Interior and Insular Affairs Committees. A call goes through to Congressman C, the acknowledged specialist. Congressman B registers her discontent, lets him know that she will oppose any such program, asks to be kept informed, and drops the matter for the present time.

This normally would be the most extreme response to word of a bureau's planning effort. A busy and active legislator with problems and programs of her own to worry about lacks the time and energy to crusade in cases like this. Most of the time Congresswoman B's response would be one of three even more limited alternatives. She might tell her staff to follow through and register her opposition, ask her staff to keep track of any such programs that may arise, or simply make a mental note to be watchful in the future herself.

The division of labor, specialization, and reciprocity that characterize legislative bodies leads to the latter kind of action, or perhaps inaction, within the legislature. And, given the extremely limited attention paid to routine matters by the chief executive, this action most often characterizes the whole of government as well. The most concerned individuals will be legislative specialists like Congressman C and the staff of interest groups which represent such directly affected parties, miners and environmentalists.

Congressman C most certainly *will* respond to the *Washington Post* item if he is genuinely unaware of the proposal. His calls, however, will not go to the White House or the Secretary of the Interior. Initial inquiries will be made with the Bureau of Mines and Bureau of Land Management, the two bureaus which should have jurisdiction over such a program. He will want answers and a briefing; and, because of his influence over program approval and funding, both will be forthcoming.

The same thing will be true for the interest groups. It is almost impossible to believe that Congressman A could inform them of something about which they were not previously aware. Keeping in touch with pending programs is one of the major jobs of interest group representatives, and they are seldom uninformed. But, if they were caught unawares, the newspaper column will inspire several lobbyists to visit bureau offices that day.

The scenarios illustrate the important thing about American politics that has been emphasized continually in earlier pages. That is, the flurry of activity over any one program normally involves only a limited number of individuals—the people whose institutional responsibilities bring them into regular contact with one another. In other words, programs normally are developed by bureaus without much fanfare, and bureaus face political pressure from only a few individuals with whom they have had previous contact.

These few people are the ones who work out the early compromises on developing programs and, as units, have been referred to by journalist Douglass Cater as "subgovernments" which operate on their own.[13] Subgovernments set so much of the direction for programs that the rest of the political system is left only to tinker with the basic design. Another, more revealing name, has been applied to this interactive network by Ernest Griffith.[14] Professor Griffith called them "whirlpools" in order to describe the centripetal accumulation of power in the hands of a few bureaucrats, legislators, and lobbyists. Within government, most of the day-to-day decisions go on within these whirlpools of concentrated activity, and nonspecialists are generally excluded.

ILLUSTRATION 3.2

INTERACTION WITHIN "WHIRLPOOLS" OF ACTIVITY

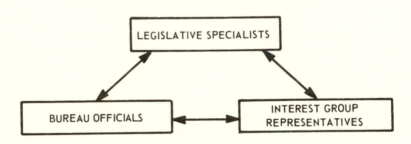

The political world of the bureau, at all levels of government, is centered within these whirlpools of activity. This explains why bureau personnel deal with fellow specialists first, and it also underscores the prominence of the bureau's political resources. On regular matters, this interaction is the routine of American politics. Other political actors are secondary in importance to those who dominate subgovernments.

A CASE STUDY OF POLITICAL INFLUENCE

This chapter has focused on the political institutions with which the bureau must cooperate. It emphasized the collective nature of executive decisions, the importance and limits of executive control of administration, and the pervasive influence of "whirlpools" of legislative and group activity. The concluding section reexamines these key points. But, instead of summarizing the material, it places it in the context of a case study of one bureau, the Law Enforcement Assistance Administration (LEAA).[15] Since this administration and its programs were created and organized together, the events being discussed apply to both.

The Law Enforcement Assistance Administration operates as a bureau within the U.S. Department of Justice. It has its origins in the Crime Control Act of 1968, commonly referred to as the Safe Streets Act. As such, LEAA's creation was just one part of a larger package, a factor that colored much of the political discussion surrounding the bureau.

President Johnson, who proposed the bill originally, primarily was interested in the whole proposal and its emphasis on federal funding. He had no special interest in either LEAA or its programs. LEAA, to Johnson, was just a necessary piece in a larger puzzle which, as an assembled whole, was designed to bail him out of one of his most pressing political dilemmas by demonstrating federal concern for the problem of crime. The "law and order issue" was, and had been since the 1964 election, one of the major political problems for the President. The losing Republican candidate, Barry Goldwater, had made it a campaign issue by placing the responsibility for increased crime and unsafe neighborhoods on Johnson and his Attorney General. Goldwater kept this criticism up after the election, and Johnson was also subjected to continual criticism by the public, the press, and Congress for "ignoring citizen safety." The Crime Control Act, as proposed in March of 1967, was a response aimed at eliminating these complaints as the 1968 election drew near. In other words, the issue was especially crucial to Johnson despite the absence of any crisis.

Johnson had only two concerns about the act. First, he wanted it passed; and, second, he did not want a harsh bill that would make him look like a Southern bigot. Law and order was, with regard to that second point, an issue associated with Goldwater and George Wallace, and Texan Johnson needed to avoid their sort of public image. Beyond those two points of direction, and partially because of the latter, White House planning was left to Attorney General Nicholas Katzenbach and his successor, Ramsey Clark. Their reputations were as ultra-liberals, and their legal philosophies were those of the social humanitarian. Both brought this philosophy to the deliberations about the crime proposal.

Unfortunately for the President, the Attorney General's directives were heavily felt in the planning. Part of this impact was due to the absence of any one bureau which could coordinate program development. Recommendations were collected from many bureaus and assembled in pieces in the Attorney General's office. But of at least equal significance was the existence of the report by the President's Commission on Law Enforcement and Administration of Justice.[16] This document, by the commission that Katzenbach chaired, served as an extremely detailed set of guidelines for bureau planners. Planning officials knew, to an almost unprecedented degree, what criteria they were to apply and how this recommendation would be judged.

This was unfortunate from Johnson's standpoint because it ultimately meant that the President totally lost control over the proposal. Clark's viewpoint, it seems, was shared by almost no one else who mattered in the fight over the bill. Congressmen, interest group representatives, and many other bureaucrats came down solidly against the act as it was proposed. Their collective sentiments were to "get tough" with crime; and they refused to accept the recommendations of the Commission Report which Clark had made the basis for the Safe Streets bill.

The first opposition came from law enforcement interest groups, most notably the International Police Chief's Association. Then Justice Department bureaucrats, including Federal Bureau of Investigation Director J. Edgar Hoover, were heard to be grumbling against it on the sidelines. Hoover scoffed at the bill's sentiments generally; but he became especially hostile to LEAA, a bureau which he claimed would become a national police force. The proposal, however, passed the House Judiciary Committee with no serious opposition or, importantly enough, strong support.

Things quickly heated up on the House floor. Opponents took over the bill's direction and interjected arguments like those made by Hoover. Before long the issues of states' rights and federalism were as much a part of the debate as law and order. Floor action was spearheaded by Representative William Cahill (R-N.J.) along with Representative John Rooney (D-N.Y.), Chairman of the Appropriations Subcommittee for Justice. They, in turn, were strongly supported by lobbyists from the Governor's Conference who were especially interested in proposed LEAA grant programs. This coalition worked well together and won over the support of most Republicans, most Southern Democrats, and many other Democrats as well. The bill was soon amended beyond recognition.

In the Senate, much the same thing happened. But the bill was still in committee when the dismantling started. Senator John McClellan (D-Ark.), Chairman of the Justice subcommittee on Criminal Laws and Procedures, was especially irritated with the proposal and led the attack. McClellan, the congressional expert on organized crime, sympathized with the states' rights arguments but he was incensed by the underemphasis on what he called "the rackets." He felt that organized crime was responsible for much of what the Commission Report attributed to social injustice, and he wanted the Crime Control Act established along his guidelines. McClellan's influence and opposition meant that the Johnson proposal had no chance in the Senate.

House and Senate changes restructured the entire proposal, and LEAA, the subject of our concern, was no exception. That organization was stripped of most of its originally proposed powers, including direct control over federally funded grants to local police. As a result, LEAA was not permitted to operate a bureau which could work to secure national guidelines for local police standards. The fears of officials like Hoover, the interjection of states' rights as an external issue, and general disenchantment with federal control of local programs led many legislators to vote to experiment with a form of revenue sharing. LEAA's programs finally were set up to turn funds over to state and local governments without restriction. The bureau became nothing more than an advisory body to assist in the establishment of state planning agencies and the utilization of funds.

This was certainly not the intent of President Johnson. The act was passed; but it was one he had not wanted, one with a tough law and order emphasis. Johnson had relied on the judgment of his advisors, and these liberals proved to be politically out of touch with reality. As a result, the "whirlpools" prevailed with an assist from states' rightists. The legislators, bureaucrats, and group lobbyists who specialize in law enforcement dominated the construction of the Crime Control Act of 1968. And the bureau that resulted was made to serve these interests rather than to reform them. As Nicholas Katzenbach later said in reflecting on the operation of LEAA, it is "almost antithetical to what the [Crime] Commission thought was important and to what the Commission thought the federal role ought to be."[17]

SUMMARY

Despite much of what is heard and read, the President and other chief executives lack much of the power people expect them to possess. This is especially true when it comes to control over the bureaucracy. If bureaus are indeed controlled, it is by specialists in Congress with the assistance of their interest group allies. Legislatures, with their division of labor in committee systems, retain a greater capability for understanding bureau operation and program proposals. But they do so by relying on the insights and opinions of individual members who "do their homework" for committee assignments.

However, it is questionable whether legislators really control bureaus. In fact, these individuals rely heavily on bureau cooperation for their own information and knowledge. If it is necessary to speak of control at all, it appears that "whirlpools of activity" control public programs.

That is, specialized bureaus, legislators, and representatives of interest groups share their own political resources in order to determine the content of legislation and the way its goods and services are delivered to the public. These triangles of government operate largely unchecked within their own spheres of influence, seldom bowing to the intervention of chief executives, political parties, or other outsiders in the political process.

4...

BUREAUS and the BUREAUCRACY

The bureau, as portrayed in Chapter 3, responds to the influence of other political institutions. That portrayal is incomplete, however. In reality, the bureau reacts to more than just elected politicians and other "whirlpool" participants. There are, in addition, complex political relationships within the bureaucracy as well. Other organizations affect bureau action; and, in turn, the bureau gains political support from bureaucratic allies for use in its dealings with the chief executive, legislators, and interest group representatives. This chapter examines the internal political world of the bureaucracy in order to explain the limits of the influence and support of the various components.

The complexity of the bureaucracy means that each bureau must deal with a variety of other organizations. Some will be working under the direction of political leaders for control purposes. Others may be parts of the bureau's own department or agency. In addition, interbureau cooperation is commonplace even when no legal ties or formal obligations exist. Regardless of who they are, these other bureaucratic institutions have a significant impact on the development of any bureau's programs.

CONTROL AGENCIES

Many governmental agencies exist because politicians fear that bureau officials might exercise too much discretion over their programs. This is especially true of the federal government, but almost all units of government in the United States have experimented with some *centralization* of control in attempts to curtail the influence of bureau officials. The usual pattern for centralizing control is quite simple and direct. The legislature or executive creates a separate organization and requires other bureaus to report their activities. This organization receives bureau reports, reviews their authenticity, issues its own compiled summary, and passes it on to the appropriate elected officials. Normally, the agency also makes some recommendations or comments about the programs of the various reporting bureaus.

For want of a better term, these are called *control agencies* because the programs they operate are supervisory rather than intended for the delivery or protection of goods and services. In a sense, they are not really bureaus as they have been discussed here. But they most certainly have a bureaucratic purpose, and they are assigned manpower and funds to carry it out. They receive ample amounts of both. For example, federally operated control agencies grew more during fiscal year 1974 than federal bureaus administering programs.

The term "control agencies" may be somewhat misleading because, in actuality, these organizations are not intended *to* control other bureaus directly. Instead they gather data and report to political authorities who, in turn, exercise control. In other words, they are best understood as agencies *for* control.

Many bureau officials claim that it is impossible to overemphasize the power some of these agencies have, however. These officials are not alluding to any legal powers that control agencies have to force bureau compliance. Control agency influence is based on the recommendations they make and the extent to which other political leaders accept their advice. If an agency's reports and recommendations are almost always followed by the President, for instance, that agency is a powerful force for a bureau to reckon with. As a result, bureau officials who need presidential support work hard to cultivate the goodwill and support of those in the control agency, and they devote a great deal of effort to preparing programs that will get a favorable hearing there.

To some degree, all control agencies have political influence. They owe their creation to a need to coordinate, and thus centralize, knowledge about fragmented bureaus and programs. This indicates that somebody is depending on them for assistance; and the more authority a control agency has to make detailed recommendations, the more others can rely on them when making political decisions.

This influence can be observed in both the Council of Economic Advisors and National Security Council. Both of these are federal control agencies with technical staffs which draw information together from throughout the bureaucracy and personally advise the President. No important economic or foreign affairs decisions are made before consulting with the appropriate agency, and some Presidents have made it their practice to accept whatever these agencies recommend. One federal agency, the Office of Science and Technology, was frequently called on by Presidents for recommendations about scientific feasibility before Nixon abolished it. While OST existed, many bureaus took special care in developing technical programs since they realized that a careful review might be forthcoming. They could never assume that the President and his advisors were scientific neophytes, easily confused by technical terms and mathematical applications. In fact, OST assistance was missed so badly that President Ford asked for its reestablishment early in his term of office and appointed H. Guyford Stever as its head.

The Executive Office of the President houses the most fully developed set of control agencies with "analytical and policy staffs."[1] Although not all of the agencies within the President's bureaucracy are of this type (see Table 1.1), several are; together they cover a variety of broad areas where policy could be formulated. While other units of government lack this diversity, many do have at least one control agency within their bureaucracy; and usually it is located within the executive office. At the state level, the most common of them are called Offices of Planning and Programming or something similar. These offices normally have responsibility for reviewing all newly proposed programs and making recommendations about how well they fit in with other state programs. Similar agencies, with the same purpose, exist at the local level in many large cities and usually are called something like the "Department of Urban Affairs."

Despite their potential influence and presence at all governmental levels, control agencies have not been too instrumental in deciding how well bureau programs match the overall set of problems facing government. Their impact in this respect appears to be sporadic and restricted to a few problem areas, like defense or the economy. For the most part, bureau programs are not subjected to the analytical scrutiny of professional staffs who apply them to a general policy. At the federal level, for instance, there is no control agency for most domestic proposals. And state and local agencies, although they appear to be more comprehensive, seldom do any more than look for a general "fit" between programs. They normally lack access to clearly articulated policy guidelines, and this makes it impossible for their personnel to examine programs any other way. In other words, their recommendations to the governor or mayor do little more than state that a particular program does or does not complement whatever else their government seems to be doing.

This lack of real influence over programs can be seen in, and partially attributed to, the financially oriented control agencies found in almost every government. These agencies, usually called a Budget Bureau or Office of Management and Budget, have been given the most authority and biggest job of any of the control agencies. But they have never paid much attention to either how well programs are meeting their goals or how efficiently the bureaus are managed. Instead, budget bureaus focus on the fiscal needs of their government and define their primary job as dividing up the financial sum that they decide is available. They ask how much money there is to spend rather than what needs to be done. Their concern has been with fiscal feasibility rather than program quality. As such, control agencies seldom aim at forcing bureaus to develop better programs. Nor do they expend much effort on developing efficient programs for bureaus within their own agency.

That does not mean that efficiency and quality have been completely neglected. On the contrary, the federal government was organized on a Planning, Programming, Budget System (PPBS) for five years, and the explicit intent of that system was comprehensive program management within the budgeting bureau. Many state governments, and even a few local ones, developed similar budget techniques. A major drawback was that program analysts never became dominant within most of these bureaus. Budget specialists, with their traditions of assembling a package, were retained and only a few new experts with a management orientation were employed. So, despite PPBS, the form and content of budgets were rarely affected.[2]

This existence of budget bureaus has undoubtedly hindered the establishment of other, more influential, control agencies. For the most part, bureaus of that sort are still the only control agencies which get regular and routine reports in standard form from all bureaus under their jurisdiction. As a result, their presence has provided political leaders with a false sense of security about the coordination of programs. Analytical control agencies at the state and local level, as a result, are only minimally staffed and funded; and they are given limited discretion over reviews. At the national level, on the other hand, the legislative and executive branches of government recognize a need for reform but direct most of their attention to modifying the Office of Management and Budget and the General Accounting Office.

Such tinkering is a natural response given the political ties that exist; OMB budgets for the President while GAO audits expenditures for the Congress. Any substantial reorganization, at least potentially, would disrupt the competitive relationship and power balance between these two branches. As long as they retain the same general structure, however, both have the ability to at least investigate how bureaus spend their funds. At least the present arrangement provides both presidents and legislators with enough information about bureaus to know whether or not their general political directives are being followed. So far, the operation of the new Congressional Budget Office has been an excellent example of this tinkering. The Budget Office neither supplants GAO in importance nor has it provided comprehensive budget figures to refute OMB.

In summary, the actual manner in which control agencies operate limits their overall impact on any bureau. Normally, a bureau understands that it must do no more than justify its budget requests. The success of the justification, rather than the proof that programs work efficiently, accounts for whether or not the budget agency will recommend bureau programs to the chief executive.

This becomes the major concern of the bureau when developing its programs with control agencies in mind. Many know that they will never be forced to account to the National Security Council or a similar organization. And even if called on, federal bureaus realize they have enough time prior to reporting to prepare their program's presentation further. State and local bureaus realize that the attention they get from the Office of Planning and Programming or Department of Urban Affairs will be important to their future, but they also know that these understaffed agencies are at a disadvantage when a bureau presents a highly organized and well justified proposal.

BUREAUCRATIC HIERARCHY

The formal organization of every bureau is structured according to *superior* and *subordinate* positions. In a word, somebody is always boss. This means that the individual occupying the superior position has responsibility over certain assigned activities, authority to command those working under him on the assignments, and rewards and punishments to hand out to his subordinates for work-related successes and failures. Work systems having such characteristics are referred to as *bureaucratic hierarchies*.

Most public bureaus have *compound vertical hierarchies*, which means that continuous levels of superiors exist within the organization, all but one of which is subordinate to one of the others. That is, there are several layers in the hierarchy. The top layer has one boss, layer two has several individuals subordinate to the man at the top and superior to those in layer three, and so on through the bottom layer where all personnel are subordinates. (See Illustration 4.1.)

Most bureaus exist within the same kind of organizational structure. So the bureaucracy is really a hierarchy of people within a hierarchy of organizations, and bureaus are the subordinate units in the chain of organizational command when it comes to control over programs. They may have subunits themselves (see the organizational chart for the Law Enforcement Assistance Administrations, Illustration 4.2), but the division of labor within the bureau usually divides up responsibility for single programs rather than assigning totally different programs to different sections. As we saw in Chapter 2 with regard to the Bureau of Mines, the bureau is one of a series of units which are part of a larger organization, the Office of Energy and Minerals, which in this case, is part of another, the Department of Interior. The Bureau of Reclamation is another example. It is part of the Office of Water and Power Resources within the Department of Interior: and the Bureau of Reclamation has several subdivisions including General Emergency, Power Planning, and Foreign Activities. Because organizations have such a variety of structures, it is impossible to generalize much more about bureaucratic hierarchy.

ILLUSTRATION 4.1
A COMPOUND VERTICAL HIERARCHY

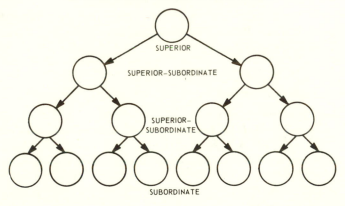

This condition is further confused by the existence of *horizontal hierarchies* as well as vertical ones. Bureaus often are assigned work and responsibilities together with other bureaus. Therefore, administrators in one bureau are frequently subject to the orders of individuals from yet another bureau.

No absolute organizational format exists for a bureaucratic hierarchy. The number of hierarchical layers varies, as does the number of units within any organization and the names of the various units. Even the specific powers of the superior unit over the subordinate differ from case to case. But these differences do not matter very much—except for their being a bit confusing. It is more important to know how an organization operates because of its hierarchy than to memorize any organizational chart.

ILLUSTRATION 4.2

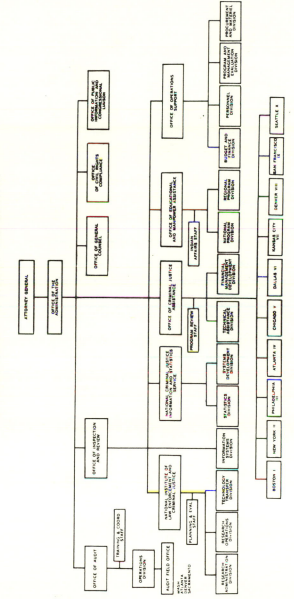

LAW ENFORCEMENT ASSISTANCE ADMINISTRATION

The word "interdependence" is the key for understanding bureau operation within the context of its hierarchy. Interdependence within a hierarchy is something that most individuals find difficult to grasp. To them, the boss should be in charge. Everyone else should be dependent on him. The logic, however wrong it might be, causes the average political observer to think of the Secretary of Transportation, for example, as *the* bureaucrat responsible for United States transportation policy. In addition, because the President appoints him, he is believed to govern transportation policy to suit a Ford or a Johnson. After all, as these observers see it, directives go downward through the command from the person in charge.

Those who share this outlook should reflect on what has been said earlier about the value of information in decision-making. After all, bureau officials develop programs. They gather and organize data. They plan. They come up with the rationale for rejecting alternatives. They make and justify recommendations. Department and office personnel listen; and, as is the case with the President or a control agency, these supervisors are at a disadvantage when it comes to distinguishing between the merits of a good program or the weaknesses of a poor one.

Hierarchy, both within the bureau and between organizational units, contributes to the advantage of the bureau in this situation. If officials at the organizational peak attempt to rely on information generated at a lower level in order to understand all the reasons for a specific program, they are bound to be very disappointed. In the first place, information must be condensed at each step. A superior could not possibly be expected to consume, or even review, all the material collected by several assistants. Thus, they request and demand summaries which necessarily provide less than total insight into the reasons behind whatever is recommended. Even a very small amount of condensing, after it recurs at four or five levels, will make it impossible for the administrator at the top to "know all the facts." This situation is made more difficult by a second factor, incorrect information. Some unintended errors, as well as intentional biasing by bureaucrats, are to be expected. Since these errors will be repeated and compounded at each level, the information reaching the top is all the more unreliable for use in directing programs. As a result, it makes little sense for ranking superiors to retain very much discretion over program development for themselves.[3] Or, to put it simply, the boss must depend on the bureau and trust its abilities. The same logic applies to the bureau head and his subordinates who do the actual development. Even these individuals can never hope to reserve complete judgment for themselves.

For their part, superiors at the department or office level have few resources to use in keeping bureau officials in line. They make recommendations about the assignment of programs, but jurisdictional capabilities generally prevail. They hire, transfer, and occasionally fire bureau personnel; but the merit system operated by civil service control agencies provides the employee great protection. Career employees know what work standards they must meet and what criteria exist for promotions. In addition, they have certain transfer rights. No one can be dismissed, under normal conditions, for failing to recommend one plan rather than another. And, even if undesirable consequences result from the plan, it is next to impossible to prove blame and attribute it to a specific person. Also, bureau superiors rather than department personnel evaluate and rate bureau employees, except for those at the very top. Since the immediate supervisor's recommendations formally guide personnel promotions and dismissals, much of the discretion that other department officials might have within the bureau is eliminated. It is, therefore extremely difficult to shake up a bureau, get rid of employees with a different outlook, or even reward those loyal to the President or department.

That does not mean, however, that supervisory units have no impact. Far from it. The department reviews budget and program requests and passes them on to the executive and legislature. A bureau with a reputation of not following along will be treated harshly; and, while department opinions can be overruled, doing so creates difficulties. Most importantly, the immediate supervisory unit evaluates the bureau head and makes recommendations for his next assignment. That is to say that the bureau head's future is decided at the department level. This provides a potent weapon, although political allies often make it a hard one to use.

At any rate, bureaus are responsible to directives from those in superior units because they respect them as arbitrators. If they fail to defer, bureau officials may find themselves without support in obtaining the programs, personnel, and funds they need. However, they pay greatest attention to the specific individuals most likely to affect the bureau's long-range future. This means that career civil servants get special respect. Elected and politically appointed bureaucrats generally understand far less than career personnel about the bureau's operation. In addition, the non-careerists, and even the careerists who move into top level positions, usually move elsewhere before they can do much harm anyway.[4]

HORIZONTAL COOPERATION

Hierarchy is not the only structural feature of importance within the bureaucracy. Horizontal communication is also a necessary element of organizational operation.[5] That is, information about directives and proposals passes sideways, from bureau to bureau, as well as up and down. However, the purpose is neither supervision as with the department, nor advocacy as is the case with the bureau. Horizontal communication exists because bureau officials seek assistance in developing their programs.

Some of this communication goes on inside the department between regular and specialized bureaus like the Bureau of Mines and the Mining Enforcement and Safety Administration. A few of these specialized bureaus are internal versions of independent control agencies, and they coordinate such requests as those for personnel or funding. In addition, they provide technical assistance and seek to secure bureau conformity to departmental standards. Many organizations also have control bureaus for legal problems, usually called the General Counsel's office, and others providing long-range planning staffs. Both of these types assist in executive and legislative relations in addition to their advisory efforts.

In terms of their political significance in the development of programs, these specialized bureaus are quite limited. Their most valuable contribution is as intermediaries who clarify directives for the bureau and programmatic plans for superiors. As interpreters, they have little opportunity to bend programs to their own liking. At most, these specialists become advocates for either the superior or subordinate position and use their intermediary positions to argue for their ally's advancement. Beyond that, they lack political resources of their own because they neither control programs nor generate new information; and they seldom gain the dependency of others.

On the other hand, some informal arrangements between regular bureaus are likely to have major effects on the design of a program. The definition of the problem to be solved, the targeting of a population to be served, the organization of the delivery system, and the determination of the amount of needed funds all are often resolved by asking other bureaus for aid. For example, if the Bureau of Health Manpower Education in HEW were to begin developing a training program for lower income minorities, its officials would probably not undertake a new survey of any kind. Instead they would turn to other bureaus which have been exposed to this problem for information. Most likely, because the program would have to be designed with its target population in mind, HME officials would go to the Department of Labor's Manpower Administration and the source of much of that bureau's data, the Bureau of Labor Statistics. They could also ask personnel from a variety of bureaus within HUD and HEW about the difficulties they faced earlier in recruiting and training ghetto residents, and they also could study these bureaus' reports on cost before calculating their own.

Information of this sort is exchanged between bureaus within departments as well as across department and agency lines. It is exchanged through formal requests as well as informally by friends who happen to be working on similar projects. Some data is obtained from bureau reports and data archives. The rest is picked up across luncheon tables, cocktail bars, and at parties. The only safe thing to say is that bureau officials will be constantly on the lookout for helpful information when a need, especially a new one, arises. And, if a lead to valuable information does come up, they go through whatever channels are necessary to obtain it. At least this situation prevails as long as making contacts is easier than collecting new information.

The importance of horizontal relationships and interbureau communication can be emphasized by contrasting this with the ones between bureaus and the organizations attempting control or supervision. In the latter case, the bureau cooperates because it must. The law requires it. Bureaus have the capabilities for developing programs because of the expertise at their disposal; and, without the force of administrative law, they would gladly do so without involving agencies who only impose costly standards on their programs. On the other hand, bureaus interact horizontally with each other because of need. Raw data, facts about social and economic conditions, information about what approaches seem to work and the like are at the heart of a bureau's needs. This material not only facilitates, in many cases, it actually makes the work of the bureau possible.

The division of labor within the bureaucracy makes this interaction essential. Education problems are clustered together and subdivided as are those in agriculture, housing, health, international affairs, and so on. However, specialization within the clusters according to such topics as higher, secondary, and elementary education does not eliminate the common elements between them. It is obviously necessary for bureaus to interact in order to share the common body of information that provides insight into what each of them is doing. If they all gathered their own data and did not share successes and failures, futile duplication would occur. And, more importantly, much more work and time would be necessary for any bureau to record any major advances in its programs.

Also, interaction must exist because jurisdiction over programs is not as easily divided and assigned as one might expect in a highly fragmented political system of operational "whirlpools." There are countless examples of program duplication, and this increases the need for the interchange of information even more. In 1969, for example, there were eight separate federal departments and agencies operating their own, uncoordinated manpower training programs for ghetto residents.[6] In addition, various bureaus within the Department of Labor sponsored at least five separate ones. There is no logical stipulation that dictates that those training programs must be considered as either labor, education, commerce, or urban development in their orientation. No clear-cut jurisdictional distinctions place them in one bureau or another, as happens when the Air Force claims bombers and Agriculture insists on autonomy in crop production research. Those two are obviously programs which fit the "heartland" of Air Force and Agriculture bureaus, but many programs exist in "no-man's land" and are hard to identify with any one particular bureau.[7]

REGIONALISM

Most bureau officials are officed neither in Washington, a state capital, or even a city hall. Bureaucrats, like the research staffs of the Bureau of Mines research centers, have increasingly moved to problem sites in order to deal with them directly. That should hardly be surprising. Wars, for example, are not fought by staying home. And there is widespread agreement on the need for dispersing bureau officials when other crises occur. Presidential campaigner Dwight Eisenhower recognized that sentiment when he campaigned on the statement, "I shall go to Korea," presumably as military commander-in-chief. Millions of average citizens have also acknowledged it by lamenting "those bureaucrats who do nothing but sit on their backsides in Washington."

A typical federal bureaucrat employed, for example, by the Veteran's Administration is more likely to find himself in a regional office (like Kansas City), district office (like Saginaw, Michigan), or branch office (like Mt. Pleasant, Michigan, or the State University campus there) than in Washington. The same organizational network of regions, districts, and branches characterizes most state bureaucracies too. Local governments, because they cover much less space to begin with, are not as decentralized in their staffing; but even at that level and especially in the larger cities and states, subdivided district operations have long been established for public safety, health, and education services. In addition, urban administrators have been moving out into neighborhoods as the idea of "little city halls" has spread in the past few years.

There are several reasons for this decentralization. First of all, most programs are meant for delivery to citizens in specific areas, and needs are likely to vary from place to place. Dispersion of personnel allows bureau officials to gather information about local needs for program development and to set up the delivery systems best suited to given areas. For instance, the Upper Peninsula of Michigan requires bureaus of the State Department of Natural Resources to plan different sorts of wildlife harvest programs than for the Detroit area, and they need very different patrol patterns to secure enforcement of game laws in each area. The second reason is that locally placed bureaucrats are more likely to recognize these differences and, as a result, incorporate them into recommendations about program needs. Thus, programs can be set up to meet local needs rather than to serve some nonexistent "average" condition within the government's boundaries. Third, these officials are likely to become more familiar with other political officials from these areas than they would if centrally headquartered. They can meet with them regularly, gain an understanding of their political goals, and, hopefully, learn to avoid the conflict that a lack of understanding often brings. Finally, program implementation should be quicker because locally oriented officials will not have to take the time to learn about the area before delivering their services. It should eliminate many errors, because guesswork is not efficient and decentralization aims to minimize it.

Of course, decentralization may not work optimally in practice. Many guesses are still made, many local problems are not understood, there are misunderstandings with other officials, and factual errors in program design still appear. Nonetheless, decentralized bureaucrats, while they do very little actual design work, contribute valuable information about what goes on in the field. Local expertise and local political contacts both are real political resources for field staff. And, as a result, these staff members are often influential in program development because headquarters relies on them.

Local staffs are never autonomous from the rest of the bureau. They are usually subjected to strict command from the central bureau staff. Headquarters tells them what information to look for, what responses to make in a certain situation, and what types of projects deserve funding. In addition, local staffs are carefully audited by headquarters. Usually, they also must submit at least large projects and expenditures to the central bureau before undertaking them. To a degree, this tight control has lessened in the past ten years as regional offices have gained more discretion. They normally are authorized to search for additional information; and, when they point out important factors that need special treatment, these are usually taken seriously at headquarters. Some regional offices even have been able to investigate and fund large projects on their own without central approval. However, practices vary from bureau to bureau; and it is safe to say that most autonomy still rests with the actual program designers and directors in headquarters.

This recent tendency toward discretion may or may not continue in the future, but the overall reliance on decentralized staff operations is undoubtedly increasing. States like Michigan are presently reorganizing their entire public bureaucracies into standard regional and district areas for the expressed purpose of greater interaction between bureaus and local residents. In fact, only a small number of states have not considered regional standardization. This same feature can be seen in the proposed charter revisions of large cities. Decentralization and local control of bureau programs were both key issues from the moment charter revision was brought up in New York City. In 1974, the new charter for Detroit incorporated decentralized administration into a city government that already had experimented with "little city halls."

The biggest and most pronounced change has come about with the national government though. All domestic federal bureaucracies either added or expanded their regional offices, under executive order, to conform to the ten standardized regions established by the Office of Management and Budget in 1972. Regional staffs, with only a few exceptions, were brought together in designated cities, and most were increased in size to allow greater responsibility. Federal Regional Councils also were formed to accommodate and encourage cooperation between bureaus in each area. At the same time, district and branch operations were standardized, streamlined, and coordinated as part of an overall attempt to develop better working relationships with state and local governments.

INTERGOVERNMENTAL RELATIONS

Although it is unclear that they ever were altogether completely independent, the different levels of American governments are becoming more dependent on one another. This has affected bureau operations. Local units, as always, are creatures of the state and exist at its discretion. The nation and states are legally autonomous, however; and each level has constitutionally assigned tasks. The national level is responsible for such needs as protection from external forces and the stability of economic conditions. The states, on the other hand, are supposed to provide individual protection and services of a domestic nature. Such services as police, highways, sanitation, education, and health care originally were intended to be beyond the scope of the national government's activity.

No such division occurs today. Extraconstitutional relationships are the rule. National bureaus, as discussed, operate programs in most domestic areas. Federal programs have reached into almost all areas of national life by justifying action on the basis of that government's constitutional responsibilities. Roads were first built, early advocates claimed, to aid commercial development and provide rapid troop movement. Intervention in schools took place to protect guarantees of civil rights.

Expansion has also resulted from other factors including the financial needs of state governments and the outright expansionist attitudes of national political leaders. No matter what the cause, however, national bureaucrats do work with officials from both state and local governments on most domestic programs. *Intergovernmental relations*, as described by Morton Grodzins, resemble a "marble cake" with the programs of one level of government intermingling and combining with those of the other two.[8]

The impact of governmental ties on bureau officials is substantial. Local bureaus must conform to whatever standards the states set; and, as a result, they frequently find themselves working to get state bureaus and legislators to change these restraints. School officials, for instance, must often plan programs within set mileage limits. This either prevents program growth or necessitates lobbying for changes in the tax limits. Or, city sanitation officials might find that state laws require them to renovate the sewage disposal system at a time when the council has just passed a budget-exhausting plan to drill a deep water well for preventing local water shortages. Do sanitation personnel convince the city council to postpone the well and conform to the law? Or do they attempt to get a temporary delay from the state? Problems of this sort are a routine part of the local bureaucrat's life and result from the restrictions established by other governments.

Similar standards are imposed on both state and local bureaus by those at the national level. Health, Education and Welfare officials, for example, demand conformity to equal opportunity and affirmative action hiring of personnel. The Environmental Protection Agency sets air pollution standards for cities to meet. At times, it appears that almost all federal bureaus have some control function over the operation of state and local governments. Quite clearly, no state or local bureau can begin the development of a new program without checking into conditions imposed from above which they must meet.

This is especially likely to be the case when bureaus purpose to use state or federal categoric grants-in-aid for their programs. Then they must deal with more than fair employment practices and the like. Money is power, the bureaucratic equivalent of the gunbarrel. Officials who want it must count on spending time with the granting bureau in order to get the funds. Granting officials check over the plan, suggest revisions, and finally approve it. Then the potential recipients must accept that bureau's program standards as they relate to job requirements and project specifications, and they must be willing to work with bureau officials who supervise the program. Normally their specifications are quite detailed and cover such diverse matters as location, number of clients to be served, safety standards for construction, unit cost, and characteristics of employees used on the project. Sometimes, as was the case with federally funded local government jobs in early 1975, the standards are so constraining that local and state bureaus will halt their participation in a program rather than meeting the criteria.

Rejection, however, is rare. In fact, categoric grants have become so widespread that it is nearly impossible to find a state or local bureau which has not entered into a contractual agreement with a bureau from another level of government. But, because money means control, these fiscal "partnerships" have created an amount of disaffection and even animosity among bureaus which receive them.

Unhappiness, in fact, has been one of the major factors leading toward regionalization of bureau operations. It has prompted bureaus to move their personnel closer to the problems in order to gain a better perspective before they define either standards or controls. Changes resulting from dissatisfaction among recipients have not stopped there, though. Some experimenting has been done with both *formula grants* and *revenue sharing*, two plans that turn specified amounts of money over to all eligible recipients without application and with "no strings attached." Bureaus using those funds must conform only to auditing and accounting standards after their use. Other programs for *block grants* have been established to turn over funds with "no strings attached" after the original proposal. This is the type of program administered by the Law Enforcement Assistance Administration, and it creates a more equal partnership. The applicant develops a program, and the granting bureau funds it after substantial review. The only requirement is that the plan be followed as it was approved and then audited by the grant maker. Other than that, the granting bureau participates only on a consulting basis and only upon request.

Any grant program affects the giver as well as the getter. Even granting bureaus are under some pressure. If others fail to respond to their programs, or if the projects they fund continually fail, the bureau will stand to lose its political support and its funds. Therefore, bureau officials do work to cultivate the good will of those with whom they must deal. They communicate regularly with recipient bureaus about the problems these officials face, and they attempt to incorporate their suggestions into the operation of programs.

Of course, the impact of local bureaus on the development of new federal or state programs is limited. They do not have the resources of control agencies or supervisory units, and local units do not generally provide the informational assistance that comes from another bureau or the regional office. Most of their political influence is exerted through the acceptance of grants and the successes local officials make of resulting programs. If a local bureau wants to exert pressure more explicitly, it must go through the political system of its own government and have elected political leaders carry on the fight. For example, the bureau might request assistance from its Republican mayor for support who, in turn, goes to the district's state representative or Republican governor. Then that legislator uses whatever resources he has to influence the bureau. Activity of this kind is commonplace, and it demonstrates that the political environment of the bureaucracy as a whole can never be divorced from the politics of other important political institutions. Both are interrelated parts of the political world of the bureau as can be illustrated by continuing the case analysis of LEAA.

A CASE STUDY OF BUREAUCRATIC CONFLICT

The conflict surrounding the Law Enforcement Assistance Administration, as discussed in Chapter 3, did not end with the enactment of the Crime Control Bill. Nor did the passage of the act finally establish LEAA's program responsibilities. On the contrary, the organization and programs of the administration have been in a constant state of flux due to bureaucratic struggles over program responsibility. Conflict has involved most of the organizational components reviewed in this chapter, and it has expanded outward into other political institutions to an important degree. Basically, the major features of this controversy have focused on the "no strings attached" nature of block grants, the regionalized decentralization of bureau responsibility, and the independence allowed state and local bureaus in using allocated funds. As a result, neither the bureau nor its programs have stabilized. LEAA's early years, in fact, can best be described as one of continuous development in its organizational structures.[9]

The reasons for this instability are many; but the first factor to consider is LEAA's unique program responsibility. Most federal bureaus, and even most new programs, place control at the outset firmly in the hands of headquarters staff. LEAA, with its block grants and state autonomy, was the first major deviant from this pattern. Its deviancy did not result from any peculiar law enforcement needs, however. Nor was it due to a concerted attack upon Johnson's Safe Streets Bill. The political influence of other bureaus and a system-wide controversy over the proper administration of grant programs were also determining factors.

Revenue sharing was one of the major debates of the middle 1960's, but it was actually little more than a mask for the more generic question of whether the state or national government could administer domestic programs most efficiently. Federal bureaus, needless to say, argued that they were best equipped to do so; and most of them strongly resisted revenue-sharing and all efforts to strip them of any of their control over grants. Their political strength, along with their legislative and interest group support, was enough to forestall proponents of state control.

LEAA, however, provided little of this opposition. The Department of Justice was a late comer to the grants-in-aid business, having administered such programs for only three years. In addition, they distributed relatively little money by comparison with the other domestic bureaus, who administered billions. This combination made Justice a bureaucratic environment without much of an interest in categoric grants. Also, the Department of Justice, as an organization, stood to gain substantially in funds, programs, and manpower if its officials would experiment. In 1968, the bureau administering federal funds under the 1965 Law Enforcement Assistance Act had an appropriation of only $30 million. Under the Block Grant Plan, this was raised to $63 million in 1969 with a total three-year appropriation (1969-1971) of $860 million.

Chances for successful acceptance of the block grant system were increased further by the creation of a brand new bureau within Justice. This bureau was staffed, not by former grantsmen, but by new employees selected and brought in to coordinate a new type of program. Therefore, their organizational loyalties and payoffs were linked to a different environment and set of tasks than those which affected the goals of most other bureau officials. LEAA employees were quite willing, in other words, to work on a program in which the states had great control.

This attitude was reinforced by the enormous organizational problem that faced Justice employees under the Johnson proposal. They would have administered the entire program for every city of over fifty-thousand population under that plan. In comparison, a more easily administered state orientation looked attractive even though Ramsey Clark resisted it. Quite logically, LEAA officials supported the state approach and were moved to further favor state control as well. This meant they would be free of cumbersome responsibilities and from much of the directive ability of a hostile department secretary as well. Having LEAA tied to the states removed a great deal of the Attorney General's potential authority.

Thus, several bureaucratic factors were important to the bureau's early development. The influence and opposition of other departments and bureaus made the Crime Control Act an excellent place to experiment on "New Federalism," as Nixon was calling it in his campaign. There was no forcing of "new tricks" on "old dogs" either. In addition, Justice and LEAA officials were to be rewarded for experimenting with this new concept. Growth, ease of program administration, and freedom from hierarchical constraints were all organizational gains.

Future development within LEAA, after passage of the enabling act, similarly was motivated by bureaucratic politics. A change toward regional approval of block grants was especially important to the organization, and resulted from dissatisfaction with ineptness in LEAA headquarters. The administration originally had a three-member board, or "troika," which was required to approve all LEAA-sponsored programs unanimously. The "troika" members, however, soon became program advocates with rather narrow and individual interests. Too often each board member approved or rejected programs solely on the basis of his interest rather than specific state or local needs of the applicant. Then a lengthy delay ensued while they sought to persuade one another to change their minds. Instead of arranging trade-offs with one another, the administrators simply tied up bureau operation. Not surprisingly, LEAA developed a reputation as a plodding and impossible bureau among those attempting to secure its grants. Its central staff was always waiting for answers before it could supply either information or aid.

This situation strengthened the regional offices and eventually led to a decentralization of the grant program. State planning agencies and their boards, in the absence of answers from Washington began to rely more and more on the staff in the seven original regions. These offices soon became the only functioning units within LEAA, as their staffs traveled around assisting state officials. Finally, political sentiment and operational reality turned against the central office. The backlog of applications in Washington, the continued inability of LEAA leaders to make decisions, the unhappiness and complaints of state officials, congressional pressures from both proponents and opponents of the organization, and interference from the Nixon White House, which was anxious to make the block grant concept a success all became too much for LEAA to withstand. Some action had to be taken to get the organization moving; and, in 1972, grant processing and approval were both transferred to the regional offices.

A key factor in this transfer was the effort of the regional directors. They actually lobbied hard for this change and the increased program control it gave them. In fact, regional directors served as the one link that brought all of these diverse elements together to pressure for the change. Regional officials talked to both state and central staff officials and promised them greatly increased efficiency in processing grants. State law enforcement officials, in turn, talked to both legislators and the White House on behalf of the transfer in order to get funds moving. The same was true of middle level LEAA staff in Washington, but they acted because they feared that their superiors were destroying the bureau.

Even that action did not restructure LEAA's operation for long. The Washington office, concerned over its loss of power, began an immediate reorganization effort in an attempt to win back resources. And, as it started putting itself in order, the central staff began to take action to regain grant authority. Headquarters officials started to meet with and cultivate the support of state officials; and they made claims that the regions exercised too much discretion over the grants they approved. Obviously, this was a situation in which headquarters was trying to take away allies from the regions.

Then, in 1974, LEAA transferred or removed all of the regional directors and their assistants. It also began taking back some of its authority over grant approval on grounds that the regions were not moving rapidly enough in disseminating funds. As evidence, headquarters pointed out that LEAA has been unable to increase its expenditures, remaining constant over each of the past three years. This lobbying, which went on in both the Congress and in the White House, reveals the tremendous amount of conflict that can go on between components of any bureau. In the immediate future, it is only reasonable to expect more bureau action motivated by that tension.

In addition to dealing with its own immediate problems, LEAA also has been affected by the actions of control agencies in developing its organizational operation. The Office of Management and Budget and the General Accounting Office have been especially noteworthy in their impact. In the controversy over regional authority, OMB directives on regionalization proved a good rallying cry for the regional office. Regional directors were able to challenge central LEAA leadership by describing how their proposed grant control would conform to the "New Federalism" of the Nixon administration. In addition, the regional directors even provided an assist to OMB when they gave their support to the decentralized control of programs. All of this made it more difficult to recentralize program approval later than it would otherwise have been.

While OMB has provided both problems and assistance, the General Accounting Office has proved to be a decided liability to everyone in LEAA. GAO has set out on a number of specific investigations of LEAA-funded programs at the bequest of congressional opponents of block grants. For example, one of their regional offices was told to search for deficiencies in the "half-way house" projects in their region. In general, GAO has criticized LEAA for violating the legislative intent of the Crime Control Act, for inadequate technical assistance and auditing, for approving underdeveloped state plans, and for a lack of interest in innovative programs. While these claims have often been used by both regional and headquarters staff to criticize one another, their combined effect has been embarrassing and somewhat damaging to all concerned. Even worse, the charges have been difficult to counter since many of them are primarily criticisms of the state orientation of the bureau, a position that is impossible to change without legislative action. But LEAA officials must still prepare programs to minimize the effects of such criticisms.

It should be evident that the bureaucratic environment of LEAA is quite complex. Most other bureaus are hostile to its operational format. As the vanguard of the block grant system, LEAA is subject to frequent criticisms from those committed to categoric grants. In addition, regionalization of programs is an issue that divides LEAA internally and subjects it to even more criticism from centralized granting bureaus. State bureaus also present problems because they match LEAA factions against one another for reasons of their own. This further heats up those in other political institutions who are already attempting to direct LEAA programs. Then, upon presidential or congressional request, control agencies step in and offer criticisms that must be answered. One of the most remarkable things is that LEAA officials have any time at all actually to develop any public programs. But that is the saga, and the dilemma, of all bureaus.

SUMMARY

The political environment of the bureau is full of bureaucrats from other institutions. Bureau officials must contend with a great many hired politicians who wish to influence and control them, as well as with the assorted legislators and interest group representatives they routinely face.

Within the bureaucracy, bureau officials must worry about five sets of bureaucratic relationships. First, control agencies have been established for designated problem areas such as the economy or science, and bureaus must report appropriate activities to them. Agency attempts to coordinate and review bureau programs can lead to loss of funds, modification of programs, or even their elimination. Second, bureaus are almost always part of a larger departmental or agency hierarchy. Requests for funds and programs must be approved at each level. Third, bureaus must coexist with one another. Programs are often shared or, more frequently, demand cooperative effort. Fourth, agreements must be reached within bureaus. Special tensions exist between bureau officials in the central office and those out in regional and local offices. Fifth, intergovernmental relations and grants programs bring federal, state, and local government bureaus together for joint projects. Officials at each level, in such cases, control various parts of a project with no one bureau in complete command.

Under such conditions, the bureau confronts a formidable task in securing the appropriations and legislation it wants. However, despite the complexity of the environment and the many hurdles which must be overcome, bureaus possess strong resources for securing what they want. These resources and the work of the bureau are the subjects of the next section.

SECTION THREE

THE WORK OF BUREAUCRACY

5...

DEVELOPING PROGRAMS
in a MAZE

Chapters 3 and 4 outlined the political environment confronting the bureau. Typically, a bureau must work its way through a host of directives from that environment before it can make its programs serviceable. But there is much more to consider. Focusing on the bureau from a purely political perspective neglects the very resources that give it the strength to dominate the construction of government programs; that is, its expertise and problem-solving ability. Those subjects are the topics for the next three chapters.

Bureaus have become important to government because elected officials come and go without institutionalizing permanent places for themselves and their successors as experts in the various problem areas facing society.[1] Many politicians lack the technical skills and analytical ability to function in such a role, and there are no provisions to insure that those who follow them in office will possess research capabilities. There are no guarantees, in fact, that politicians who secure office will have any interest in becoming experts. The history of the congressional committee system, for example, shows that politicians like Jamie Whitten develop expertise through their own hard work. There are no apprenticeships for passing on accumulated knowledge about special areas of interest. Nor, since our elected institutions formally operate by sharing decision-making in all problem areas, does such a system appear likely ever to emerge. Executives and legislators become specialists only when they, individually, choose to do so; but societal problems demand constant and steady vigilance. For these reasons, no modern government can be without its career professionals who are hired to remedy this electoral deficiency.

POLITICAL CONCERNS

In effect, bureaus walk a tightrope while developing programs and plans for the future. They must maintain bureau credibility while being politically responsive. No bureau, quite obviously, can resist all the political directives it faces. But, at the same time, no bureau can afford to continually shift its position on programs according to the whim of political sentiment. To do so is an admission that the role of expert is not really important to government. If that is the case, there is no reason for elected officials to request the assistance of bureaucratic specialists, because it would be commonly known that their testimony is subject to the controls of whoever exerts the most pressure. If such a bureau existed, it would lack *legitimacy*, or credibility.

Bureaus, as a result, must appear to be politically responsible to programmatic suggestions and also fiercely independent in pursuing the right answers to questions about societal problems. The bureaucrat who cultivates a successful image follows leads but does so while investigating other possibilities. An LEAA official neatly summarized the importance of this middle ground in commenting on the political problems of his bureau: "For the past six months we've concentrated only on our concerns, we've lost sight of our objectives. The trouble is that nobody believes we know what we're doing."[2]

This does not mean that bureau officials will propose unpopular programs at all costs. Of course not. Political concerns are too real for that. It only means that bureaus cannot afford to be pushed in whatever direction political influentials want. They must often resist, and resist hard, but never to the extent that it threatens money, jobs, and program approval. And never to the point where the bureau makes permanent enemies for itself by appearing to be self-righteous and unreasonable.

Acknowledging the need for balance, however, is not the same as defining limits for political responsiveness. What is optimal attention to such concerns by one bureau probably would be inappropriate for another. It depends, for one thing, on who is talking. Some bureaus need not face the pressures of a strong regional office, state government officials, or an interested president. Others must adjust to these intervenors frequently. Similarly, the bureau's latitude varies with the resources of those attempting to exercise control. The Central Intelligence Agency, for example, has less to worry about from sympathetic Senator John Stennis (D.-Ala.) than most bureaus do in their relationships with legislative specialists. LEAA, on the other hand, must constantly direct a portion of its programs toward organized crime in order to avoid the the hostile intervention of the already suspicious Senator McClellan.

Another important variable affecting a bureau's control over its own programs is the sophistication of its research skills and data. Some programs, by the nature of the problems they are to solve, deal with more complex, technical questions than others. This, of course, often gives a bureau an advantage over others which must base their programs on more subjective information.[3] Unless cost factors are exorbitant, a bureau has an easier time presenting an expertly developed, and largely irrefutable, program if it is scientifically based, proven, and tested against clearly definable objectives. The military, for instance, finds it more difficult to sell Congress on the need for manpower training than it does new radar systems for its B-52 bombers. It can demonstrate comparative deficiencies and improvements for the radar system by measuring basic capabilities of each against the other. However, no one can prove that the training program will guarantee future employment or increased job efficiency. Such research findings are found to be "soft," or largely subjective, due to the many assumptions that must be included in their calculations.

Soft programs, and the bureaus which rely on them, will be the most susceptible to political interference. Congressmen will find the justifications for those programs understandable and easily placed into the value-oriented frame of reference that all individuals possess. Thus, legislators can quite comfortably challenge requests of this sort.

What options does a legislator have, however, when confronted with an Agricultural Research Service report that recommends mandatory fuel allocations to fertilizer producers by showing dramatic crop production losses that would result without the program? None! He votes for it. Likewise, a governor finds it hard to argue against pollutants found in his state's rivers by the Environmental Protection Agency. But he can disavow the applicability of LEAA suggestions about the specific need for state law enforcement planning standards by citing his own information about Iowa's peculiar population pattern.

Soft programs are those based upon evidence that is difficult to quantify in absolute terms. The projected results of a particular bomb dropped on a city leave little room for questioning the precise meaning of what is to occur. But softer programs are planned using factors that are not easily held constant. Researchers find it extremely difficult to predict how a family will behave when welfare benefits are increased, since they are unable to know and control whatever else in the family's immediate environment influences behavior. On the other hand, agricultural specialists do know what environmental features affect corn growth; and they can plan for possible variations in weather, disease, and pests accordingly. It should be clear that the presence of any human factors in its programmatic projections will present the bureau with the greatest difficulties. Thus, social programs and those emphasizing administrative reforms normally find the greatest challenges, while those proposing changes in such things as military hardware, space exploration, agricultural production, and highways are questioned primarily in terms of government's ability to pay.

BUREAU ORGANIZATION

A bureau's need to legitimize its technical and problem-solving capabilities explains why internal organization is the first step in developing its programs. Before it can begin to plan, the bureau must be able to plan. And it must be able to demonstrate this capacity to those who review its work. As a result, a bureau like LEAA subdivides itself into units such as the National Institute of Law Enforcement and Criminal Justice and the Office of Criminal Justice Assistance.[4] The institute is responsible for developing and suggesting new law enforcement programs and for carrying out the bureau's research. It is also designed to communicate new ideas generated elsewhere inside the bureau to potential supporters in the criminal justice community.

Obviously, even this specialization leaves the bureau with a complex workload. So to accomplish their goals, bureaus subdivide even further. To do its work, for instance, the National Institute of Law Enforcement and Criminal Justice operates four specialized components: Research Administration, Research Operations, Technology Transfer, and Planning and Evaluation. (See Illustration 4.2.) Subdivisions like these provide the bureau with an opportunity to identify and employ specialists whose permanent assignments provide them continuous opportunities to sharpen their expertise and add to the credibility of the bureau.

Since technical analysis is now at the heart of goverment programs, it is rare to find any bureau without research divisions similar to those of LEAA. But, because planning needs involve more than just research skills, most bureaus also have other units within their organization to supplement their research arms. Auditing and inspection offices are both usually maintained to review internal, or "in-house," activities to ensure the orderliness of program operations including research. Also, several specialized divisions often exist to deal with legal problems, congressional liaison, and public relations.

Offices of this type are intended, at least in part, to provide or gain some degree of support for program development by applying their own expertise to bureau problems. For example, an auditing office provides researchers with information about the precise budgetary guidelines that should be followed if they want to avoid antagonizing those attempting to exercise financial control over the bureau. And legal offices can supply statutory information about legal questions that the bureau might best avoid. On the other hand, public relations offices and those for congressional liaison are essentially lobbying efforts whose jobs are to win friends for the bureau's new programs. But even these offices often detect information of political importance and relay appropriate messages back to the planners for their consideration.

All of this internal organization is basically a task for the bureau itself. Except for authorizations for funds and manpower, the process doesn't depend on the involvement of many external political forces. Unlike major reorganizations of departments and agencies, the President and Congress are generally not involved. Even when supervisory bureaucratic institutions must approve the organizational structure, there is seldom much resistance from above, since the superior units themselves are rarely affected. Thus, bureaus are reasonably free to adapt to the needs of their environment when deciding how to organize.

The same holds true when bureaus reorganize. They carefully scrutinize their organizational problems and deficiencies and propose corrective measures in the form of new structural arrangements whenever they might be appropriate. The 1974 reorganization proposals of LEAA are a good example. At that time, two problems plagued headquarters staff: congressional criticism of the quality of bureau programs and their own inability to control and coordinate regional operations. To correct these conditions, the administrator appointed an investigatory management committee whose task was to analyze the possibility of alternate arrangements for developing new programs.[5] The report of this internal committee pinpointed both those areas where change might be helpful and those areas which should remain untouched.

Despite the internal nature of planning for organizational capabilities, the presence of nonbureau forces can never be forgotten. At the very least, the bureau is attempting to thwart possible criticism of its actions. Or, as was the case with LEAA's reorganization plan, it proceeds in order to negate criticism. Oftentimes, however, the need to expand its financial base while reorganizing necessitates the more direct involvement of other political decision-makers for support. The emergence of the U.S. Army Special Forces as a major bureau of the military provides an excellent illustration.

The Special Forces, after nearly ten years of stable operation, played only a small role in Army affairs well after the outbreak of hostilities in Vietnam. In fact, there was no clearly defined contribution that the

Special Forces could make to the unfolding war effort, since it was little more than a holding company for Army experts in various forms of unconventional warfare. However, the commander of the Special Warfare Center at Fort Bragg, North Carolina, recognized the potential of transforming this array of experts into a force capable of excelling at guerrilla tactics.

This transformation required two things: increased funding and the political support needed to procure it. To obtain these related necessities, Special Forces command began an elaborate publicity campaign to advertise its troops as an elite specialized force able to go anywhere, anytime, and do almost anything. At the same time, Special Forces troops were being coordinated so as to combine their scattered talents into a single unit. In addition, minor training reorganizations were carried out in an attempt to bring as many as possible of these specialized skills to each Special Forces soldier. The intent, first of all, was to convince the Department of the Army that it had a potential superforce of supersoldiers if it would only support them.

Soon the Army General Staff was attracted, and various Army forces assisted the Special Forces' drive to publicize itself as Jet Age replacements for the marines. Their efforts culminated in a personal visit from President Kennedy to the Special Warfare Center, where he was treated to a full-scale demonstration of freefall target parachute jumps, scuba diving, and linguistic exercises in which one demonstration team spoke to him in almost forty languages. Then Kennedy was presented with a green beret and the commander's request that Special Forces troops be allowed to wear this uncommon piece of attire as their own "badge of courage."

Special Forces began to expand rapidly after Kennedy's visit, and their troops were given the bulk of assignments for preparing increasingly demanding ground warfare programs in Vietnam. The command had effectively convinced the Army of its capabilities and the merits of increased support. But, of equal importance, it won an ally in the White House who brought the bureau increased attention and stature in its fight for appropriations and assignments. Only after that success was Special Forces put into a position to translate its organizational talents into battlefield heroics.

FACT FINDING

For many readers, *"fact finding"* might appear to be a summary of what bureaus should do after they have organized. But the term fails to describe even the entire planning process of the bureau, let alone its concern with putting programs into operation. In essence, fact finding is only data gathering, just one component of planning. Briefly, it can be described as the task of laying out of information about societal needs prior to deciding what action is required.

Data gathering, however, is enormously more complex than might be imagined. Its ease most certainly cannot be compared to collecting eggs in a basket or picking wild berries. Bureaus neither collect whatever is neatly arranged before them nor do they file away every piece of possible evidence that might be available. There is just too much information in the world for that. Any bureau following such a strategy would be quickly inundated no matter how large its research capabilities and its computer's memory.

Therefore, the fact-finding job of the bureau begins with a decision about selection. What facts matter from among all those available bits and pieces? As a result, bureau officials spend much of their time deciding what is irrelevant to their problems. This does not mean, however, that bureaucrats perform their work by throwing out all data with which they disagree. On the contrary, as can be seen from the following example, they strive to identify appropriate data amidst the disarray.

In the mid 1960's, officials from the National Institutes of Health were anxious to study the combined effects of poverty and malnutrition. They were reluctant to conclude anything from the available data; and yet they chose not to undertake a more detailed study from among the identified population of urban poor. Why? Wouldn't it have been easy to take the poor and rapidly complete an examination of their nutritional intake and health conditions? Certainly it would have, but other facts made these officials question the validity of such a study. For instance, other available information led them to believe that the urban poor were not particularly bothered by hunger problems because of the presence of uniquely urban welfare programs. Moreover, it was increasingly evident that urban residents did not constitute, as had once been assumed, even the majority of citizens living in poverty. Because of this, NIH researchers felt that the rural poor, who were not identifiable through presently accumulated data, should be included and studied since these individuals were the most likely to suffer from malnutrition.

Searching for applicable data leads most bureaus great distances and to great costs. In order to report on the nutritional status of the poor, for example, health care officials finally conducted a comprehensive National Nutrition Survey in order to include all important variables and populations.[6] Unless bureaus are willing to search out information that is hard to find, difficult to recognize, and oftentimes cleverly covered up, they can never hope to justify those programs they have been organized to handle. In other words, bureaus must engage in both *selective* and *extensive* search to accomplish their goals.

To achieve this necessary precision and breadth, bureaucratic fact finding must be just as concerned with scientific *methodology* and *technique* as it is with substantive information. That is, bureaus must develop the proper tools to answer their questions as quickly and accurately as possible. Data gathering no longer proceeds on the basis of discussions between informed experts who share their opinions. Most bureaus use systems analysis to help determine whether or not all important factors have been considered.[7] Likewise, many bureaus are capable of conducting their own sample surveys to measure basic needs as well as public opinion.[8] Some have even set up controlled experiments to generate data about the likelihood of one program succeeding and to ascertain what variables account for success.[9] A list of research methods used by government bureaus could be expanded indefinitely.

In order to utilize such techniques, though, bureau decision-makers must first devote time and attention to defining the nature of the problems that confront them. It does little good to have research facilities, experts, and equipment if the bureau has no awareness of what it is trying to find. Sound research begins with ideas about what to look for, where to look, and why the expected is likely to be found.

To this extent, no programmatic fact finding can begin in the dark. It must have direction. But how do bureau officials know where to begin? The answer to that question has at least as many answers as there are possible political forces to affect the bureau. And it has many more because the bureau can—in fact is likely to—set its own guidelines and investigate in the manner its officials choose. Bureaucrats, as has been seen, are the government's resident experts. As bureau employees, they should be attuned to pending social changes and failures in ongoing programs. This makes them, more than anyone else, likely candidates for suggesting what bureaus should search for.

INTERPRETATION

The work that confronts a bureau after data has been gathered is usually more perplexing to its officials than any other part of their job. This is because no particle of information means anything before it is related to some broader environment. Everyone sees this in their own lives as they observe their surroundings. One's personal assessment of a new highway is based on such factors as new ease in getting to the stadium, the loss of a hundred feet of front yard, and the panorama of Mack trucks replacing the wooded lot next door. Public officials, however, usually are not as familiar with the environment that surrounds most programs as they are with their own neighborhoods. Consequently, bureau specialists must go to great lengths to explain the data they have gathered. Or, to put it another way, they must correctly *interpret* the meaning of their data and explain whatever implications it has for the problem being considered. Interpretation also involves relating all the diverse facts and data to one another. For instance, education officials might try to demonstrate how improper nutrition, rather than simple hunger, accounts for educational failure. Interpretation, therefore, involves systematizing data as well as explaining it.

Much of the frustration that comes from the bureau's interpretive role results from the reluctance other officials feel about being led to conclusions. Politicians like to believe that they can, indeed they should, make their own decisions on issues. Accordingly, bureau supervisors and elected officials can be comfortable with a presentation of data but be very touchy about accepting judgments about its meaning.[10] Because of this, politicians often paraphrase Dragnet's Sergeant Friday by asking for "just the facts." But, when left with just the data, these officials are bewildered, confused, and even angered by numbers and projections with which they have no familiarity. The most confounding thing about the situation is that there is no solution. Different recipients have different tolerances for interpretive material; yet none of them can get along without some assistance. The only recourse that the bureau has is to present its case as matter-of-factly as possible and attempt to show quite specifically how their interpretations derive from their findings. That is, bureau officials must demonstrate that their personal values are not the driving force behind the conclusions they draw. This is the key to the bureau's success in its political dealing and compromises.

The data that has been gathered is often as frustrating as the politicians with whom bureau officials must deal when it comes to interpreting findings. In a very basic way, much of what the bureau finds does not lead very far toward absolute conclusions. Bureaus often lack definitive data.[11] What, for example, does the Michigan Department of Natural Resources conclude about the presence of the chemical PCB in fish taken from Lake Michigan waters? They know the chemical is there in detectable amounts. They understand what PCB does to rats in a laboratory who ingest large amounts of it. And they even find evidence of its presence in people who have consumed Lake Michigan fish. These are facts. However, does this mean that the fish are a real hazard to humans? Is it possible for people to consume enough of the chemical to affect their health? Can that interpretation be made from accumulated data? Dilemmas such as this are typical of the ones that confront the bureau. The evidence is so scanty. The answers could be so damaging.

Because of situations like the PCB deposits in fish, bureaus always are in a search for better data. Yet they cannot just sit back and wait for the arrival of perfect answers. Problems will get worse, conditions further aggravated, or a crisis might even come about because of inaction. Therefore, specialists oftentimes find themselves in the uncomfortable position of interpreting facts to officials who want or demand immediate answers even though bureau data leads to less than absolute conclusions.

There are many reasons why this occurs. Sometimes the right facts lie hidden among so many others that only the interrelated jumble can be detected. For instance, we know that poverty exists because certain people lack money. But what, specifically accounts for their inability to generate an income? There are many theories, but no hard evidence. Frequently the data is available but irretrievable because of the way it was collected and stored. Internal Revenue sources certainly could have located accumulations of low-income citizens through tax records if records were filed for such a purpose. The records are unavailable as a survey of the poor, however, and government officials believed incorrectly for many years that the urban areas were the primary trouble spots. In other cases, so little is known about the basic problem that there is no guide for directing officials toward the missing data. Waiting periods for new breakthroughs in knowledge are especially commonplace in the application of hard sciences and engineering to programs involving missiles and space exploration. The above explanations, and many others like them, only suggest that the research capabilities and the intuitions of bureau experts are imperfect. Problems persist indefinitely as a result. This disconcerting fact must be faced by all bureaus as their personnel seek to explain the need for publicly supported programs.

RECOMMENDATION AND ADVOCACY

Bureau officials who interpret data must be able to go at least one step further and recommend what action government should pursue as a result of its findings. Someone is bound to ask "What should be done?" And no one can afford to be in the position of a DNR biochemist telling the legislature or governor "You decide what to do about people eating contaminated fish. You've seen the weaknesses of our data. Make up your own mind. I don't know." Obviously that bureaucrat never existed. Responses of that sort undermine the legitimacy of a bureau and cause everyone to wonder why the state supports the particular division.

Since the bureau is expected to be of assistance in sound program development, it must be willing to offer a detailed plan once its officials start to discuss societal needs. Their plan should recommend a course of action based on the immediate problem, "Ban the fish from commercial consumption." It should take related but lesser problems into account: "Allow continued sport fishing, but issue warnings about regularly eating these fish. That is, more than once a month." It should also take into account the consequences of its actions. For example, "We must provide state compensation to those commercial fishermen who will be put out of work." Finally, the completed plan should contain provisions for enforcement, for an approximation of cost, and for a predrafted enabling act. A plan of this dimension provides government with the greatest possible contribution from its specialists; that is, if the bureau is correct and if it avoids political conflict.

Avoiding conflict and being right are ideals, and ideals hardly ever exist. Bureaus count on some conflict since their programs usually disadvantage someone. More frequently than not, the bureau must use its ability to make recommendations as an additional opportunity to present its case and show its expertise. In those cases, data, interpretations, and recommendations will all be part of the same package and build on the previously stated components without relying exclusively on them for support. For example, the DNR might present its data on PCB in fish and then emphasize the crisis this situation could cause. Instead of openly worrying about whether the data presents any certain hazard, department representatives would proceeed to argue that the appropriate bureau within the department is fully prepared to take action and should do so in order to avert any future problems. In short, the department promotes the whole program on which it is prepared to act, not just a few accumulated facts.

Bureaus follow strategy of this sort in order to gain an advantage over the opponents they expect to meet. By taking the initiative and presenting a detailed program, the bureau is able to exercise an important degree of leadership on the issue being discussed. At least, from the bureau's point of view, their program is the starting point for further deliberation; and it has the advantage of being derived from the data that serves as the basic definition of the problem. Even if the bureau's data is weak, it is likely to be more thorough and better detailed than any that may come from alternative sources. Moreover, by linking data, interpretation, and recommendations together, the bureau implies that the definition of the problem leads to a feasible response that its personnel are capable of implementing. After that position is advanced, it becomes very difficult for opponents to argue against the bureau because no one else can make a better case for or against its capabilities than its own officials. These points can best be illustrated by applying them to the example of the Department of Natural Resources.

With regard to the PCB issue, the joint presentation of data and interpretation defines the issue as a health hazard in the minds of all those listening to the DNR. In addition, a program has been suggested. From then on, no opponent, such as commercial fishermen, can attack the DNR without refuting the health charges. Yet they are entirely unlikely to produce any counterevidence allowing them to challenge the department's interpretation effectively. Therefore, lobbyists for the fishing interests are placed in the position of arguing against DNR recommendations with no supportive evidence of their own. If they hope to save the fishermen's source of employment, their best strategy might seem to be acknowledging the presence of PCB and proposing corrective programs such as water treatment, treatment of fish catches to reduce chemical effects, new fish stockings, or the development of an immune fish species. Realistically, however, bureau officials are likely to argue that the state lacks the ability to pursue these alternatives. Or they might argue that the costs of reorganizing to meet one of these alternatives are prohibitive. In either case, the fishermen will find it extremely difficult to debate DNR capabilities with its own specialists. If they hope to gain any benefits in this instance, fishing interests will be best advised to seek increased compensation for income losses. They could probably win there, since bureau spokesmen have already agreed to the stipulation in principle and are likely to be cooperative in order to end the confrontation.

It should be obvious to the careful reader that bureaus seldom take a neutral position on their recommendations. Instead, they play an advocate's role and promote what they have planned. It would indeed be foolhardy to think that bureaucrats concerned with legitimizing their place in the political system would not fight to protect a plan they believed in.

There are other important factors that lead bureau officials to become advocates, however. In the first place, bureau personnel often have a vested interest in a program's passage. The interest may be in increased funding, jobs, and promotions; it may simply entail continuation of business as usual and the preservation of existing programs.[12] More frequently, though, bureaus develop an organizational commitment to proposed programs because these have been planned with their own capabilities in mind. Planning, like many other enterprises, is the art of the possible; and bureaucrats really mean "Can we do it?" when they ask "What is possible?"

This is an extremely important consideration, since most program developers later face the task of implementing their plans. Therefore,

bureaus must ask several organizationally relevant questions as they prepare recommendations based on their findings. To what extent must we
reorganize to handle the program? Can our present staff do it? What
extra funds can we expect within the bureau for the program? How will it
affect our capabilities in regard to our other programs? And, finally,
there is the big question. Can we accomplish the goals established for the
program? If that question cannot be answered positively, the future is
risky and the bureau will probably back off. No bureau that desires
continued support can afford to fail and be labeled incompetent.

Given those considerations, the enthusiastic support of bureau officials
for their proposals is easily understood. The weeks of preparation for
meetings with budget officers and Appropriations Committee members
become obviously more important if the bureau's need to win is
analyzed.[13] The personal and organizational costs that are at stake under-
line the significance of both good strategy and avoiding conflict. Since
bureaus pay a high price when their opponents force changes and
compromises, the importance of interest group and legislative supporters
is also clear. Bureau officials gain a great deal by compromising with
"whirlpool" partners early in the deliberative process. By doing so, they
avoid later conflicts with specialized decision-makers and simultaneously
gain additional advocates for their program's difficult journey through
the political maze. But bureaus can only form those necessary alliances
and gain political successes by developing capable organizations which
produce reliable data and well-planned programs that others will accept.

SUMMARY

Bureaus that are successful in their political dealings gain their success
because of their credibility. And this credibility, or legitimacy, is obtained
through the bureau's research skills. When funds can be obtained, bureaus
secure them on the strength of reasoned, scientific information. Under
normal circumstances, those bureaus that get what they want operate
programs based on hard data.

To become successful, bureaus first organize themselves to do research
and answer the difficult questions that plague elected politicians. Today's
bureaucracy, as a result, has become heavy with problem solvers, data
analysts, and computer specialists. Most bureaus operate several offices
of their own to house a complete contingent of these needed specialists.

Research-oriented bureaus are best understood as fact finders set up
to identify problems within their jurisdiction. As government's resident
experts, specialized bureaus then go on to develop programs. Program

development involves putting gathered data together, interpreting that data, defining and explaining its implications, and then recommending a course of action for government to pursue. While doing this work bureaus actually draft, or assist in the drafting of, most of the legislation that Congress considers. However, bureaus can seldom end their development work at that point if they wish to see their ideas become law. In most instances, bureau officials become forceful advocates for their proposals who must follow the bill through to avoid misunderstandings and crippling amendments that could change the program's impact.

6...

OPERATING GOVERNMENT PROGRAMS

Implementing programs presents bureaus with a complex set of problems that few observers have studied in detail.[1] Too often "implementation," the carrying out of a legislative act's intent, is considered a leftover of the decision-making process. Observers who are inclined to separate "political" from "administrative" decisions are especially likely to draw that conclusion and ignore the impact of whatever occurs after the enabling act's passage. Those sharing this orientation tend to equate implementation with simple distribution; that connotation suggests a rather clerical sorting system which automatically assigns the benefits that the law specifically provides.[2]

Nothing could be a more inaccurate description of implementation, however. There is nothing automatic about putting programs into effect. As noted in Chapter 1, enabling acts only generally outline the means for obtaining a program's goals. After this initial agreement is reached and funds committed, bureau officials are left with great discretion in the delivery of goods to clients and the establishment of intended service facilities. In fact, bureaucrats make extremely important decisions about who will and will not be rewarded at several different times prior to the actual distribution of benefits. In addition, they must interact with innumerable other officials who influence such allocation. Quite clearly, political factors are as pervasive at this stage as they are during program development.

MORE PLANNING

The first task that confronts any bureau after its programs are assigned is the accumulation of additional information and more planning. Neither the procedures for assigning programmatic benefits nor the methods for their enforcement are normally established by legislative order. Bureau officials also are left to determine who is eligible for their benefits from among the many applicants who might apply.

Bureaus, without a doubt, have planning needs to meet which are extremely important to the accomplishment of a program's goals even after the basic designs are set into law. For example, decisions made during implementation can make it extremely difficult or extremely easy for recipients to claim benefits. Or they can establish waiting periods and cut-off dates for eligibility. Enforcement standards can be made lax to encourage participation and innovation, or they can be made so rigorous that few will elect to utilize the program. Such standards also limit the use of machinery to encourage caution, but they can also allow widespread usage under various circumstances and risk equipment loss and failure. Most significantly, however, implementary decisions can determine whether or not the program will ever reach its target clientele or accomplish the goals for which it was initially intended.

Both the magnitude and impact of planning vary greatly from program to program. A 1974 act, for example, authorized continued research and construction of the B-1 bomber for the Strategic Air Command. Under such a legislative directive, previously designed airplanes are to be built in line with announced blueprints and costs. The Air Force and its contractors need only to engage in the demanding technical work of making B-1's fly safely and perform efficiently. Other programs have no such specific charges, however. For instance, the National Highway Traffic Safety Administration is authorized to implement motor vehicle safety programs in order to reduce the severity of injuries in automobile accidents.[3] Under those broad guidelines, that bureau originally was able to mandate both interlock seat belt systems and air bags for automobiles without specific mention of either by Congress. In fact, the Safety Administration's authority to promote Federal Motor Vehicle Safety Standards was so broad that it could force auto manufacturers to produce *and include whatever passenger* safety features its officials found necessary. Obviously, this authority gave NATSA more leeway than SAC had with the bomber; and, as a result, their planning and data collection needs were quite different.

Much of the information that goes into implementation research, however, is not freshly collected. By necessity, bureaus must have information at their disposal during its developmental stage in order to make a program operative. Without such data, officials could not answer questions about *programmatic costs* and the *likelihood of success*. And without this information, executives and legislators would balk at turning over funds for any program's completion because it could turn out that costs might continuously increase without producing noticeable success. For this reason, aerospace engineers most certainly addressed questions of costs, capabilities, and efficiency during early development of the B-1. That information was necessary in order to advance arguments for the replacement of the B-52 although Congress and the President were already prepared to accept air power and strong national defense as basic societal needs. But they had to judge the B-1 in the context of whether or not its particular weapons advances were worth benefits from other programs that had to be sacrificed to obtain the weapon. Given the scarcity of financial resources and the nature of political deliberations, SAC had to be prepared to present this type of information prior to receiving support. To at least some extent, the same is true for any bureau promoting new programs.

Since a good deal of data is not new, its planning application is what varies from development to implementation and distinguishes the two stages. During development of the B-1, for example, engineers attempted to establish an estimate of the cost of producing safe, efficient flight. However, implementation needs dictated that they translate their original calculations into design features of the plane in order to make it stand up to the rigors of a variety of flight conditions. This situation existed because delivery of the product, rather than the previous need for political acceptability, becomes the bureau's desired end after an act is approved.

These two contrasting goals can lead to a disparity between what the bureau promises to develop and what it ultimately provides. This result is especially likely to occur if the bureau is hard pressed to gain approval and must work hard at cutting costs or providing maximal benefits. Many of these estimates are unrealistically shaped by the pressure the bureau faces in gaining approval. Since estimates have often been inaccurate, more and more government programs are being developed with prototypes, or experimental models, which actually can be used to demonstrate that early planning promises will come about. Using prototypes, a bureau allocates designated research funds to construct an instrument or system for testing; and then its officials modify it after conducting research on its performance in various contrived settings. Only after substantial data about how the program could be put into effect has been gathered does the bureau request full authorization of the program. Under such circumstances, all parties to the decision gain advantages. That is, bureau personnel have more sound data to use in advancing their cause; and supervising cfficials can be more confident that their investments will succeed.

Weapons programs and those using technical hardware, almost without exception, have now begun constructing prototypes prior to requesting legislative approval. This allows bureaus to demonstrate that the plane actually does fly faster, the computer does speed up computation, and vehicles do use less energy. Even with such prototypes, however, bureaus are unable to show how hardware systems will bear up in actual, everyday use. In addition, they usually must rework original projections in order to deal with the problems of mass production and the final details that vary when the final products are applied in different settings.

More difficult problems face bureaus whose programs are softer. The success of a prototype welfare system, for instance, is not easily assessed and measured.[4] And very little research money is available to experiment with the distribution of welfare payments and other social services because government, as a whole, has been unwilling to turn over large sums of money to produce very uncertain results.[5] Also, bureaus often find that clients behave differently in test settings than they do in actual life.[6]

The need to develop programs which achieve their original goal is especially great in these nontechnical areas. In the past, even the most carefully designed and thought-out welfare assistance plans were largely guesswork in their development. Bureaus dealing with human resources find it extremely difficult to plan with delivery as their primary objective because they know so little about the likelihood of their client's responses. Other bureaus like the Law Enforcement Assistance Administration face similar dilemmas. Only their role as a grant allocator makes their job even more difficult. LEAA certainly cannot go out and survey individual community needs before determining its own requests for annual appropriations and program continuation. All this must come later.

As a result, the planning that accompanies implementation is, to some degree, the key to success for all bureaus if they are to meet program goals. Many planning features must be postponed until the time for delivery. In brief, implementation is the stage where bureau officials discover whether or not their projected plans are detailed enough to get the airplane off the ground and to the target or the payments disbursed to those who need them.

THE FOCUS OF IMPLEMENTATION

Implementary planning is necessary because various settings are almost never alike, and different clients rarely have the same needs. As a result, when a program goes from the developmental stage to implementation, there is a special need for careful analysis of the different environments in which the programs are delivered on a piecemeal basis, as *projects*. That is, a program's products are not all sent out, prepackaged, from central headquarters. Only such assignments as mailing social security and revenue sharing checks free bureau officials from the arduous task of making the program's promises of benefit to the local setting. For other bureaus, implementation means deciding where near Boston a missile silo should be located, which of two potential freeway exit placements will cause the least environmental damage, or whether or not the Vine Street health clinic needs to spend its limited funds on a heart resuscitator.

A bureau's job at this point is to ensure that specific applications are derived in a practical manner from already developed programs. Military officials, for instance, must make certain that the "ideal placement" for a missile installation is not a swamp or a peat bog, a site that could conceivably be projected by headquarters personnel who formulate general location plans for all east coast missile sites based on prevailing winds and distance from population centers. Or, a bureau must decide if the Vine Street area's population contains a sizable number of potential heart attack victims without ready access to a fully equipped hospital. If City Hospital lies ten blocks away and the clinic specializes in minor disorders, it makes little or no sense to purchase a heart machine simply because the law allows it.

The need for local study is incumbent on even those bureaus that operate with the most detailed central plan for project completion. When the B-1 becomes operational, SAC bomb wings will still have to determine altitudes, routes, and defensive tactics when they have to reach targets designated by higher echelon officials. Such questions will all be dependent on weather conditions, the location of defense installations, and such other variables as the success of prior attacks on the target and its defenses. The workload of federal housing officials in the 1950's and early 1960's provides an example of the enormity of local study. Even though housing officials were criticized for over ten years as being unconcerned about individual community needs, site selection and feasibility studies still averaged well over six months each. This was in spite of the few decisions housing bureaucrats faced since they constructed, almost exclusively, large highrise apartments in isolated residential clusters.[7] The fact is that even deciding where in the ghetto to build takes time.

Although the necessity of planning is readily apparent, its absence often seems more observable than its presence. The Army, for instance, commissioned its most costly tank during the Vietnamese War; and its prototype seemed adaptable to various environs when it traveled rapidly over land and floated quickly across deep rivers. However, the tank never saw military action in Vietnam. In fact, the experimental model sank and was lost irretrievably in the swampy mire of the MeKong Delta. Afterwards, the vehicle was designated as inappropriate for project involvement for Southeast Asian programs. Other highly tested programs have suffered similar embarrassments. In early spring of 1975, Pacific-based U.S. Marines practiced for months and received daily briefings on plans developed for the evacuation of cities in Southeast Asia. Yet high officials of the evacuation program reported to Edward Kennedy (D.-Mass.), Chairman of the Senate subcommittee on refugees, that "half the Vietnamese we intended to get out did not get out and that half who did should not have."[8] Kennedy's subcommittee staff concluded that the plan was "poorly implemented and undertaken with little command control in the field."[9]

The implication of all of this is that planning and even more planning does not necessarily bring about programmatic successes. Ridiculous errors are made and will undoubtedly continue to be made because bureau officials and engineers, like everyone else, are sometimes incredibly short-sighted. Rivers and swamps are not easily confused, but their differences can be overlooked with ease even when it affects a multimillion dollar tank program. The hope must be, however, that a greater emphasis on planning will minimize errors of this kind; and, in addition, it must be hoped that a more detailed emphasis on analyzing local environments will lead to flexible programs allowing greater latitude for project variation in the future.

Factors other than just human frailty account for many errors also. Organizational capabilities play large parts; not only during implementation, but in all phases of planning as well. Bureau officials often think *incrementally*.[10] That is, bureaucrats modify previously learned experiences to fit new problems which confront them.[11] Tank manufacturing companies, for instance, use old construction standards derived from models designed for African deserts and, consequently, overload vehicles without considering the consequences. After all, as bureaucrats see it, no problems resulted before, and it appears to make good sense to follow successful applications. Or, in a different situation, settlement officials rely on their own past involvement with programs for East European refugees and fail to address the immediate problems of displaced Asian peasants who have very different needs.

The lessons that bureau officials must learn in order to avoid such errors are difficult ones: (1) look at the present, (2) closely examine the specific locale and its environs, and (3) focus on the needs of those particular clients that must have the program here and now. The difficulty inherent in these considerations exists because attention to detail is costly. Personally, it is easier for bureaucrats to rely on general lessons learned through years of experience. The actual delivery of projects becomes much more costly to them when these officials increase their own expenditures of time, energy, and effort for new investigation. Also, by increasing investigation, the bureau is likely to encounter increasing political pressure when programs that clients know are available and expect to receive are delayed. Still, however, the need to escape from the mistakes of incremental thought during implementation has led to a greater concern for local fact-finding in recent years. Reform has resulted because the effects of errors are increasingly generating political pressures upon bureaus anyway; and the resulting costs are often more burdensome to bureau officials than those of increased planning.

There is a second organizational problem that is more widespread and less easily resolved than minimizing incremental decision-making. This problem concerns the limited specialization of bureaus. In many areas, perhaps most, bureaus are almost entirely unprepared to study client needs because they are poorly equipped to examine human motivation and plan for peoples' responses. Housing officials find it easy to become experts in construction techniques and land use, for example, but they find it much more difficult to determine whether a group of clients has the background necessary for utilizing certain facilities in a project. Or they find it hard to recommend one style of housing over another on the basis of the need for integrating nuclear families. Even harder is the task of assessing the price the bureau can afford to pay in order to obtain this goal. Since the biggest charge leveled against highrise public housing is that it is "unlivable," all of these considerations are especially important ones. But what does "unlivable" mean? And why is this housing that way? These are extremely hard questions to analyze because the subjective values of bureau planners are so easily incorporated into their responses.

Answers to similarly complex questions confronted the U.S. military during the evacuation of Saigon and other Asian cities. Marine Corps units knew how to get helicopters to points within the cities and back to the ships. They understood what types of rocket attacks evacuators could face and from where the attacks might come. In short, the marines were on top of their field of expertise. Yet each project failed to deal effectively with the confusion, terror, and violence of the fleeing residents.

These individuals' human reactions were not part of the plan for evacuation; and no organizational responses were ready to meet them. In this case, the military units had capabilities other than the ones needed for an important part of their assignment. To an extent, the absence of these capabilities explains much of the failure reported to Senator Kennedy.[12]

From an organizational perspective, problems of this sort persist because bureau personnel become competent in their assignment's technical aspects and little else. The government maintains housing specialists, guerrilla warfare specialists, health delivery specialists, and those for thousands of other societal needs. Yet there is no Federal Bureau of Human Relations, nor are there many "people specialists" with dominant positions in other bureaus. Even if there were, however, it seems difficult to believe that the problem of planning for human responses could be resolved altogether. Behavior specialists, or social scientists, certainly can do much to predict personal reactions under defined conditions. And they can effectively give advice about what conditions to emphasize and which to avoid. But even these experts would be hard pressed to plan methods for control that would eliminate fiascos like the Saigon evacuation or for making a highrise project a healthy living environment. The most that could be expected from social scientists would be some help in coping with an unhappy situation. Evacuators could be made aware of trends to watch for; and housing personnel would be taught to identify resident needs for minimizing boredom, loneliness, or the likelihood of crime.

Even those contributions would be welcome ones which, too often, are unobtainable given present research capabilities. In order to avoid errors, bureaus must develop behavioral research skills further. But that is no simple task. First of all, researchers in the area must show what kind of help they can provide to the successful implementation of public programs. Beyond that, however, technical experts must accept the behavioral specialist's skills as an additional input to decision making; and, in so doing, they must give up some of their own personal influence over programs in the process. Until these things happen, a great many bureaus will find it very difficult to implement projects with a variety of client needs actually in mind. And programs will fail to be thoroughly planned because of it.

COORDINATION AND IMPLEMENTATION

The presence of many interacting political forces during implementation is another important reason why planning often seems absent. In reality, no bureau is left on its own to put programs into effect. They can only take the lead in doing so. As noted in Chapter 1, bureaus must satisfy many of their political supporters during implementation. But decisions to construct an air base in a particular district or rush through a grant to a legislator's favorite mayor are really the least burdensome of the pressures bureaus face. Even though these responses often are contrary to planned goals, a bureau normally finds them harmless to long-range plans and seldom too disruptive. The individuals making the demands, after all, are usually allies who have worked with the bureau and understand its basic goals. In addition, the committee hearing and accompanying meetings provide sufficient opportunities for bureau personnel to pick up cues as to what these other participants want and incorporate the details into the plans prior to implementation. This allows bureau officials to minimize disruptions at this stage.[13] While exceptions to the above generalizations to exist, the bureaucratic morass described in Chapter 3 proves more frustrating to the bureau that wants to get its various projects under way.

Bureaus never enjoy unrestrained freedom from other bureaucratic institutions because programs are bound to overlap. At the very least, programs are tied to preceding programs and whichever bureaus were involved with them. For example, if war breaks out in Latin America in the 1980's and B-1 bomber squadrons respond, their successes will be determined by more than the Strategic Air Command's ability to plan localized air strikes. SAC efforts also will depend on how effectively the plane was designed and built in the original program that provided the weapon. And, to a great extent, the raids will be a result of the B-1's failure to deter war in a program for peaceful coexistence. "Peace is our Profession" indicates the role that manned bombers are supposed to play in providing a balance of power to avoid international conflict. These simple illustrations show the central position of the B-1 in three separate and distinct programs; and components like the bomber relate many programs to others throughout the bureaucracy in this way.

Bureaus can also affect one another's work when their programs become involved with one another during implementation. One of the most common examples is a bureau's need to conform to Affirmative Action guidelines established by the Equal Employment Opportunity Commission. Officials from Community Development and Planning must file reports with EEOC about several aspects of employment including the percentage of minorities employed in the construction of local projects. If the commission's standards are not being met, however, the two bureaus will work together to find solutions. At the extreme, a project might even be halted until the building contractors hire more blacks or do whatever else is necessary to satisfy the commission.

Although shutdowns are relatively rare, one bureau's actions can delay implementation and inconvenience another's clients. For example, a construction delay could move the completion date for a reservation community center past the date for the tribe's annual festival, an act that could cause a decline in anticipated tourist attendance and a corresponding decrease in revenues earmarked for furnishing the center. Or, more seriously, a construction delay in a housing project could cause further shutdowns if the project delay makes it impossible to complete work by winter. If the city has a scarcity of low income housing and an increasing migrant population, a situation of this sort might cause both hardship and increased expenditures. The bureau in charge of the project might have to find other living facilities, spend additional funds for rent, and force its clients to spend many months in overcrowded and inadequate housing.

Situations similar to those above can come about even in crises. Delays are not restricted to settings where bureaus interact on relatively small projects removed from the eyes of the public and elected officials. The mishandled evacuation of Saigon provides a striking illustration. In Saigon, the U.S. Marine Corps was to take charge of the evacuation, but the corps was under the command of the State Department embassy, specifically Ambassador Edwin Martin. Although marines in the Philippines carefully developed their plans for bringing in transport vehicles, Vietnam-based marines were not directed to do so by Martin, and neither were State Department personnel. Nothing was done until a few days prior to the actual evacuation, when local marine officers took it on their own to implement plans. To coordinate efforts, marines who had developed the initial plans in the Philippines flew to Saigon for planning sessions in civilian helicopters, wearing civilian clothes to protect their identity from State. These clandestine meetings were all that enabled participating marine forces to begin the evacuation with some confidence that it would be completed. But even when the marines judged that actual evacuation was overdue and local conditions were critical, Martin still did not order it. As a result, marines started evacuation without State Department consent; and it was two hours later when the ambassador gave the word. During this time, the marines used commandeered taxi limousines as escort vehicles. Marine planners had expected that Martin would delay too long and earlier had obtained the vehicles, painted them black, and equipped them with blue lights and forged State Department decals.

The conflict and distrust between these two organizations explains much about the evacuation's failure to achieve its goals. Human uncertainty, as noted earlier, was an important factor. But the inability of the marines to plan openly and at length for the actual assignment probably was even more critical. Successful implementation depended on marine intelligence and minimizing potential risks through careful analysis. Yet the embassy only served to obscure things; and Martin's hindrance serves as an example of how to make a bad situation worse by denying a bureau knowledge and support. For State Department employees in Vietnam's Delta region, it will remain as an especially lucid example. Those personnel seemingly were overlooked in the hasty withdrawal; they found a boat and drifted out to sea, where they were discovered.[14]

Although the examples above might seem complicated enough, problems of implementation are far more complex when they involve many bureaus simultaneously. The Normandy invasion of World War II and the redevelopment of Pittsburgh's riverfront are two examples of programs constructed from other programs. Normandy involved not only bureaus from every branch of the United States military, but civilian bureaus and those from allied countries as well. It would be most surprising if even the commander, General Dwight Eisenhower, knew every bureau that was involved. In the case of Pittsburgh, city redevelopment officials designed a program on the basis of what local, state and national bureaus could contribute to the renewal effort. For the most part, implementation was little more than a collection of grants-in-aid from federal bureaus and the attached conditions of the grants dictated much of what Pittsburgh was able to build.[15]

As would be expected, programs involving different governments are the most difficult to implement. There simply are more bureaus involved and each of them has some jurisdiction to watch over and protect. Jeffrey Pressman and Aaron Wildavsky detailed the hazards of federal interaction and aptly titled their text *Implementation: How Great Expectations in Washington are Dashed in Oakland.*[16] Their Oakland case study examined several projects of the Economic Development Administration that were intended to provide jobs and income to area residents. However, the projects resulted in almost as many bureau conflicts and delays as individual jobs. One of the projects, a marine terminal, was finally constructed; but it took nearly five years of negotiation even to let the contract. During that period, EDA plans first were delayed because the Port Authority couldn't secure the funds to develop plans and specifications for their own involvement. Then, after federal loans were advanced, the project was postponed while the engineer hired by the Port of Oakland with the loan went to work on other assignments. Delays also occurred because the

U.S. Navy protested dredging operations, the Federal Aviation Administration was slow to rule on air safety aspects of the terminal, the Bay Area Rapid Transit District caused the Army Corps of Engineers to refuse the Port's dredging permit, and the General Accounting Office challenged the amount of the project grant.

When bureaus implement their programs with those from another government, they must deal with new political problems as well. Bureaus with offices in foreign countries must concern themselves with the culture and norms of their host; and their elections, economic conditions, and revolutions will be subjects of immediate concern. The same hold true when bureaus work intergovernmentally with one another on domestic programs. A federal bureau constructing local projects must be attuned to local interest groups, citizen demands, and those of local politicians. The construction of highrise public housing projects in Chicago in the early 1950's is a prime example. One of the reasons housing officials went to Chicago was because local politicians, including Mayor Kennelly, were not opposed. Officials in other communities were less neutral. Then, when several community interests became opposed to the project's implementation, plans were changed to forestall opposition from the mayor or council. The highrise concept was agreed on to placate northsiders, projects were located apart from residential neighbors to quiet southsiders, they were built within walking distance of downtown to please business groups, and so on. Implementation was little more than a series of compromises to avoid opposition.[17] To some extent, it must be this way in every setting; but it is especially likely to be the case when citizens have their own officials to turn to and mobilize against a bureau from another government.

It should be clear by now that implementary planning is more than just the accumulation of additional evidence. Beyond the problems of gathering facts are those of coordination. Bureaus must coordinate their plans with other bureaus and take into account whatever political conditions they find in the locales where bureau officials wish to build or establish delivery systems. Bureaus have no other choice than to cooperate, because these organizations and individuals have the authority and power to keep programs out or, at least, seriously delay their entry.

EVALUATING PROGRAMS

Many politicians, citizens, and even program analysts seem to believe that the delivery of public programs constitutes some final act. There is some merit to this position since recipients are often permanently affected by either what they receive or how they are treated while receiving it. It has been argued, for instance, that welfare bureaus treat their clients without respect and cause them to lose their dignity and self-esteem.[18] That may well be true; but the argument presents an inaccurate picture of all welfare officials purposely directing themselves toward the debilitation of the poor, which is hardly the case. It must be kept in mind that the programs were designed and passed for assistance, not persecution. If clients are made to lose self-respect by their treatment in welfare offices, it is the delivery that is wrong and the implementors that are to blame. The result cannot be treated as a blanket condemnation of the whole system of welfare programs.

The significance of the example lies in the failure of implementation. Obviously, if recipients feel degraded, goals are not being effectively met. And when such results occur, the work of the bureau is incomplete. Its officials must discover what is wrong, find out how to correct it, and then proceed to deliver benefits in some better fashion.

At any rate, implementation is not a final act. It leads elsewhere. In Chapter 1, the cyclical nature of programs was noted. Programs are developed, implemented, and then *evaluated*. After that, modifications are made at either (or both) the development or implementation stages in order to correct whatever errors were discovered. Then the cycle continues. There are, as a consequence, very few concluding acts of a bureau. The actions of most bureaucrats, most of the time, are part of the cycle.

The reason for such a condition is the long-range nature of government programs. Very few are meant to conclude within one or two years of the enabling act. In fact, bureaus normally plan programs in periods of five years, and twenty-year projections are common. While these plans can be altered or eliminated by Congress when it is time to renew or refund them, reform is not an annual or even biannual possibility. It has been found, for instance, that upwards of 80 percent of the total dollar requests for programs in the combined budget of the Department of Health, Education and Welfare are uncontrollable. That is, these outlays have been removed from the control of the President and Congress by previous legislation, and it is up to the bureaus to keep spending.[19]

Because of the long range nature of public programs, and because of their renewable nature, evaluation is necessary for survival as well as efficiency. They must be, since sooner or later bureau officials will be forced to demonstrate that their achievements over the years included more than alienating large segments of the population. If bureaus are not involved in correcting their errors, they can only expect to face a sound questioning of their expertise and a loss of legitimacy.

Historically, bureaus have always been involved in evaluations. Colonel

Custer's command of the Seventh U.S. Cavalry is a much discussed case and so are innumerable other battles that have been refought on the gaming tables of various military academies. Currently, the Office of Management and Budget and other control bureaus engage in systematic assessments which are used with the more subjective judgments that chief executives, legislators, and their staff employees form from their daily observations. These external judges have made it imperative that bureaus examine themselves in order to answer those who question their performance.

Today, most national and state bureaus are organized with at least some concern for evaluation and employ officials with the ability to systematically measure program successes and failures. Others, including many local bureaus, in even small governments, contract with professional evaluators for the same purposes. And, as would be expected, many bureaus get by without any systematic appraisals but still gather some data to justify their program's existence. The latter type of bureaus seem to be an increasingly small minority, however. Elected officials have demanded more thorough accounting from bureaus in the past few years.[20]

It is essential to remember that the political consequences of evaluation are crucial to the bureau because of its commitment to its programs. As a result, ensuing reports are intended, at least in part, to justify a bureau's past efforts. While bureau officials work to show that their programs make sense, provide benefits, and cost a fair amount, these are not cut and dried questions to answer. As James W. Davis wrote, it is a common error "to think that efficiency, economy, and rationality are values shared by all."[21] In fact, these cannot even be values defined similarly by all.

Several factors affect evaluation and determine its content. What was being measured? How does this relate to the total program? What do the findings mean? Who did the work? Why did they do it? And who within the bureau is being affected by the report?

A hypothetical example of the Law Enforcement Assistance Administration demonstrates the impact of these variables. In the first place, LEAA officials can elect to evaluate several different phases of their operation. They could determine their success in getting federal funds to cities for police work and find that only a small percentage of funding goes for administrative overhead. This can be determined by running a simple audit, and the conclusion would be judged as a measure of efficiency. Instead, however, LEAA economists could study the use local police forces make of federally funded equipment; or sociologists might examine comparative crime rates in funded communities. The first report might show bureau success because of high utilization of equipment, and the other might suggest bureau failure by detecting increasing crime rates.

Does the administration undertake all three studies? They may; but, on the other hand, one evaluation might be avoided if it could possibly cast a negative reflection on an important and well-liked bureau official. Normally, LEAA would be expected to avoid one particular measure of success, the one showing failure. If the evaluations are all made, though, are they all released? All could be used effectively for internal modifications perhaps; but the one indicating failure would never be voluntarily submitted to legislative committees or the press. That is, it would not unless one faction within the bureau wanted to embarrass another. Are these three evaluations enough? Do they allow judgments on both developmental and implementary aspects of the program? Evaluations commonly fail to challenge early assumptions around which the programs were designed, and the first two appear to be no exception since they focus on implementation. Have the specialists looked at enough indicators of success? Or are other areas neglected because of the limited expertise of auditors, economists, and sociologists? Also, were the judgments of these individuals about success and failure meaningful or arbitrary? For example, to what does the percentage of administrative costs compare? Did police departments need to use the equipment, or were their actions wasted effort? Did crime increase for economic reasons beyond the control of LEAA? All these and perhaps a hundred other questions underscore the significance of Davis's statement about values.

Conditions of this sort are not easily avoided. Many programs do not have specific goals that can be easily identified for measurement purposes. For example, how does a bureau evaluate the success of weapons in deterring war? Is it sufficient to claim that hostilities have been avoided? That tells nothing about what might have occurred without those defense expenditures. In addition, the need for political compromise makes it unlikely that there will be uniform agreement about what a program's goals ought to be. A bureau's complete and detailed analysis of its work as its officials define it will never please everyone. There will always be charges that one social need or another was ignored and another overemphasized. Even if programs are designed with evaluations in mind, charges of this sort are impossible to eliminate. At best, a bureau's professionals can design indicators of what they believe should correlate with the attainment of their goals.[22] But convincing everyone that these indicators are valid is an impossible task.

In summary, it must be concluded that a bureau's self-assessment of its programs will never perfect them. From a political perspective, evaluations are too crucial to the bureau to be something other than a justification of the programs that it wishes to keep. But methodological reasons are just as important to this imperfect result. Some questions cannot be answered by applied social science, and others can only be tentatively argued. Even if bureaus made the extraordinarily costly effort of systematically studying the effect of every decision made in a program's construction and delivery, this condition could not be avoided. Still, however, evaluation is a crucial aspect of any program, because it leads to modifications in design and bureau behavior.[23] And, since bureaus need to prove their worth by providing real benefits, evaluation is the stage that needs refinement because it promises real dividends to consumers as bureaus work to make delivery more efficient.

SUMMARY

Bureaus must implement programs as well as develop them. That is, they must deliver the goods and services provided for in the legislation establishing the program. But this is no simple task because not all of the answers about how to deliver program benefits are considered in the development stage.

Most of the work that goes on at this stage involves planning and coordinating individual projects. No two settings for delivery are alike, and these different settings must be carefully studied to ensure that appropriate recipents get what they are entitled to. Even though implementation makes use of a great deal of earlier gathered data, much of it must be gathered anew. And a great deal of new analysis becomes necessary in order to correct errors in judgment and design from the development stage. This is perhaps the most critical step in the bureaucratic process, since bureaus find it comfortable to tinker with old methods of delivery and previous ways of doing things. Too often, in the haste to get on with the job, bureau officials make very minor design changes rather than redesigning a new delivery to better serve a unique group of clients.

Oftentimes, this minor tinkering goes on because it involves far fewer risks of offending the bureau's political allies or further irritating its foes. Changes must be explained and excused to individuals and groups who had reached an understanding of how the program would work. The greater the change, the more the political danger to the bureau.

Programs must also be formally evaluated to determine whether or not they deliver what was originally determined as necessary. Bureaus undertake most program evaluations on their own and report them to Congress and appropriate executive agencies. Because bureaus are committed to their programs and have a great financial stake in them as well, proposals for abolishment seldom come out of these evaluations. However, evaluations provide a good opportunity for bureaus to suggest modifications and thoroughly document and explain the need for changes. So, if a program is to be significantly altered, it usually occurs after an evaluation rather than during delivery.

7...
BUREAUCRACY'S IRON GLOVE:
Regulation

Although only seven of the federal government's administrative organizations are referred to as Independent Regulatory Commissions, all bureaus, by necessity, regulate because of their programmatic involvement. Without direction and control, the goals set for any program are impossible to meet. And regulations provide the directive means toward programmatic ends. They are simply the rules that are intended to bring order and predictability to the administration of public programs. Regulations exist to allow both observers and participants in government to know what steps to follow, when to take them, and what to expect by doing so.

In the broadest sense, regulations are a necessary part of every imaginable step in the process of developing and delivering programs. There are rules governing jurisdictional questions, proper identification of program needs, steps to follow in recommending action, service delivery, client relations, and information requirements for evaluation. However true that may be, regulations are often defined more narrowly. This is especially likely to be the case when bureaucracy becomes a subject of political concern. Usually, in referring to regulations, most political commentators mean the regulatory powers available to bureaucrats for controlling the allocation of program benefits. These include the general procedures for distributing benefits, definitions of eligibility for recipients, and specifications of the conditions under which provider-recipient transactions take place.

By interpreting regulations this way, observers move away from a concern with the orderliness of an entire program and define the need for regulation only as the program directly applies to its recipients. From this viewpoint, bureaus regulate because there is some clientele-related need for control. A private firm is required to meet construction standards in the goods that it sells to government; or a local government must provide a percentage of matching funds and construct the facilities for a community center in a specific type of location in order to secure funding from a federal bureau. Those are examples of rules imposed by bureaus that would usually be recognized as regulations. So is setting rates for a public utility or limiting the types of items that can be purchased with federal food stamps. In assailing the "overly regulated society," most critics of bureaucracy would ignore a rule that specifies the maximum number of cases that can be assigned to a social worker, the requirement that military personnel complete a study course in race relations, or an order for bureau officials to divest themselves of investments that could present a conflict of interest. These examples are not seen as regulations because no citizen is immediately assisted or burdened by them.

To a great extent this distinction between regulations related to the direct allocation of goods and services to clients and the other rules of bureaucracy makes little sense. Rules that do not directly affect citizens or a program's recipients are still intended to protect or provide controls because of their impact on the delivery of goods and services. Regulations that bring internal bureaucratic order are still designed to make programs more effective in meeting their goals whether or not anyone outside of the organization is ever aware of them. The overall purpose of all rules is essentially the same—to bring order and better serve society as a result. A second reason for not distinguishing between types of rules relates to their origin in the planning process. In general, regulations are only an extension of the research that goes into the development, implementation, and evaluation of any program. Rules are set after environmental needs and related problems are identified; and they constantly are subject to change as new conditions arise or corrections are discovered.

However, there is one important reason for making this distinction. It allows for examining regulation apart from the rest of the work of bureaucracy. Regulation, as defined from this narrower viewpoint, can justifiably be given special consideration because the specific rules affecting delivery give bureaus their legal authority to coercively enforce the compliance of those using or covered by a specific program. Research skills only give bureaus the influence that comes through persuasive ability; but, in the area of directly interpreting and controlling the use of government programs, they have formal power to actually distribute and redistribute a large portion of society's wealth and resources. This chapter focuses on regulation because it is essential to understand the nature and extent of this "absolute power" in order to complete the picture of how bureaus operate and ultimately affect us all.

FORMAL POWER

In regulating the use and application of public programs, bureaus are following the mandates of the enabling legislation that created those programs. But, in terms of legal doctrine, they have a vast amount of discretion because enabling acts may be as nonspecific or indirect as can be imagined. According to the courts, "Congressional delegations are designed to allow agencies to develop and implement solutions; the legislature can neither foresee what actions the agency should take nor constantly revise the mandate as conditions change. To force Congress to act otherwise is to ask it to perform an impossible task and, therefore, to invite chaos . . . (T)oday it seems clear that Congress constitutionally is not required to do very much affirmatively . . . (T)he Supreme Court apparently has concluded that Congress is free to identify the problem . . . and then go tell the agency merely, 'go solve it.'"[1]

As a practice of American government, the delegation of open-ended formal powers to the bureaucracy is neither a time-honored tradition nor a recent procedural revision. It results from the pre-World War II attitudes that emphasized positive, affirmative steps by government to contribute directly to the well-being of individual citizens. That philosophy articulated the belief that law, both legislative and judicial, "evoked a system or rigid constraints that paralyzed initiative and prevented effective action to solve the problems of society."[2] If bureaus were to successfully serve the needs of clients, they needed to be free of burdensome formalities and undue legalisms which would only thwart or delay their efforts.[3]

The growth of bureaucracy since the 1930's has been, as a result of this now prevailing governmental attitude, more than increasing size and capabilities for problem solving. Bureaus also have enlarged their regulatory authority and their impact on the lives and livelihood of those under their jurisdiction as they have escaped from the confining restrictions of legal codes.

Often the regulatory solutions advanced by bureaus come close to total dictatorial control without the semblance of any legislative action related to the issue at hand. An excellent example of a legislatively unencumbered organization is the Michigan Department of Natural Resources and its many bureaus. DNR bureaus have been delegated vast discretion for any policy decisions related to the protection of fish, wildlife, and state forest as long as they secure the approval of the department's director and its governing board of citizen commissioners. Still other bureaus within the department have similar blanket authority for environmental protection and land use. This wide range of responsibilities gives the

Michigan DNR an incredible ability to affect an almost unlimited number of interests in that state.

A review of the major decisions rendered by DNR bureaus in one recent two-year period illustrates the economic impact of the department as well as its great ability to disrupt social conditions. During that time, a decision was made to ban gill net fishing on the Great Lakes. That decision forced several commercial fishermen to close their businesses. Another decision ruled that Native Americans were to be prosecuted for any violations of current fish and game provisions, regardless of any treaties to the contrary. This too reduced the earning ability of several state residents, all low-income minorities. Game management specialists were responsible for a third judgment allowing hunting of antlerless deer in the Upper Peninsula. That decision aided some businesses and gained the favor of downstate hunters who vacation in the northland during deer season; but it enraged a large segment of UP residents, who perceived critical shortages of female deer in the region. Another wildlife decision made by fisheries experts continued the costly salmon programs for the Great Lakes and, in so doing, negatively affected those with a financial or personal interest in inland stream property. These residents lost out because the DNR expended funds that otherwise could have been used to stock their waters up to past levels. But, even more critical to some stream enthusiasts was the impact the huge annual salmon spawning runs had on stream habitat and the damage created by the great influx of salmon-seeking fishermen who overcrowded the small rivers each spawning period.

Still one other set of regulations handed down by the DNR affected an even broader spectrum of the state's population than all the previously mentioned decisions. In this instance, the department determined that one section of an oil-rich area of state forest could be opened to limited drilling. These regulations ruled against environmentalists, who wanted to ban all drilling in order to protect a rare local elk herd and, at the same time, their industrial opponents, who wanted open drilling in the whole forest area to increase short supplies of fuel in the state. In each of these cases, DNR officials made important allocative decisions about who received what state benefits on the basis of their own regulatory authority. They did far more than just research solutions and advocate the alternatives of their choice.

The delegation of such broad authority is not uncommon. It is not, however, the norm either. In fact, most bureaus are usually given more specific assignments through the enabling acts assigning them programs. For example, legislative provisions usually direct that a bureau shall provide low-income housing for the needy. Or a bureau shall make hydroelectric power available to the citizens of a designated area. Or a bureau shall construct and operate a missile defense system and await presidential orders prior to any deployment. Those are more typical charges. Bureaucrats more commonly have less discretion than Michigan DNR officials. In most cases, bureau regulations are limited to such things as a definition of "needy" or a determination of the price various consumer types will pay for governmentally provided electricity.

The Bureau of Community Planning and Development within the U.S. Department of Housing and Urban Development provides a more typical example of the bureaucracy's regulatory power. CPD decisions determine, in intricate detail, such things as the number of housing units that can be provided over any one time period in one location and whether or not specific categories of families will be able to claim them based on income and the number of family members. Its regulations are more like those DNR decisions which allow only certain widths of roads to be cut into the state forest or ban noise levels over a certain decibel rating.

Any copy of the *Federal Register*, the daily regulatory tabloid of the federal government, provides readers insight into the power of bureaucracy. Two things are evident in these printed regulations: the broad discretion exercised by those doing the regulating and the enormous detail that normally goes into bureaucratic rule-making. In a typical set of regulations, the bureau defines what is permissible under the law, what requirements participants must meet, and what conditions must be present prior to approval. In a set of regulations for Housing and Urban Development's bureau for Community Planning and Development, for example, the regulations state the role to be played by areawide planning organizations at the state level, the environmental requirements applicants must meet, and the overall requirements for housing and land use elements of any approved project. They also quite specifically define who will be the organizational participants, what procedural requirements exist for application, the provisions for citizen involvement, and the focus for applicant negotiations with the department.

Even though bureaus like Community Planning and Development do not possess the potentially broad authority of the Michigan DNR, their effect on people's lives is no less great. They only lack the ability to exercise total control without legislative direction. CPD and bureaus like it make momentous decisions about whether a family will be able to move from an overcrowded, unsafe tenement or about what quality of housing facilities government will provide. In effect, housing officials decide the extent to which government will ensure safety, promote community interests, and provide a healthy environment. Bureaucrats unquestionably decide much about the quality of life available to many Americans even when the legislature actually makes the decision about how much money will be available and for what purposes it will be allocated.

RULE MAKING

Bureau rules result, in one sense, from internal study and analysis that goes on within the organization. This is particularly the case for *procedural rules*, which spell out the bureau's methods of operation, and for *interpretive rules*, in which the bureau officially elaborates on how it interprets its mission or its enabling acts. However, officials are also legally subjected to the input of interested parties prior to the formal establishment of any regulation specifically distributing a program's benefits to general categories of citizens or otherwise determining its impact on the types of individuals, groups, and organizations to be affected. For example, a hearing was required when it became necessary for bureau officials administering the Fair Labor Standards Act to determine which types of workers employed by the canning industry were covered by the statute. Such regulations are referred to as *substantive rules*, and bureaus usually must hold an open hearing before they become official.

For federal bureaus, the Administrative Procedure Act of 1946 makes it necessary to "publish an advance notice in the *Federal Register* announcing the proposed rule-making, afford interested persons an opportunity to participate through submission of written data, views or agreements with or without opportunity for oral presentation, and publish the final adopted rule 30 days before its effective date."[4] Although many variations exist, similar restrictions apply to the substantive rulings of most state and local bureaus. In some specific cases, at all levels of government, a very few bureaus are also required by statutory law to do the same for procedural and interpretive rules.

Requirements of this sort have been imposed on bureaucracy because of the quasi-judicial role that bureaus have assumed as a result of their regulatory responsibility. In effect, designated officials serve as both judge and jury to those seeking the rewards of public programs or potentially being punished by them. It is, therefore, imperative that bureaus gather as much relevant information as possible before decisions are made in order to avoid mistakes in setting regulations; and it is equally important that efforts be made to inform those affected by the program as to their potential benefits or responsibilities. It would neither be wise to limit the gathering of information that might be helpful for a program's successful operation nor fair to impose secret restrictions on clients. Both would run contrary to the reasons for increasing the potential authority of bureaucracy in the first place. For this reason bureaus often attempt to hold hearings on procedural and interpretive matters even when they are not required to do so.

"Holding a hearing" prior to a bureau ruling can mean many things in terms of operating format. As long as the informational purpose is served, almost all practices can vary. The most formal interactive setting, referred to as "rule-making on a record," is very rarely employed. During this type of hearing, involved parties testify and are cross-examined. At the conclusion, the ruling is based on facts and legal judgments resulting from the presentations. The lack of flexibility in rule-making that characterizes these settings and the corresponding prohibition against the bureau generating additional information make these tedious hearings unpopular among bureaucrats whose choice it is to select the form of hearing. In most instances, bureau officials opt for open hearings where potentially involved parties are invited to testify before those who will promulgate the rules. Such hearings are voluntary both in terms of who appears and what use is made of the material presented. The popularity of hearings of this type is easily explained by the control bureau officials exercise in their conduct. Depending on the bureau's choice, testimony may be a direct interchange of comments or it may be restricted to either limited oral statements or even written comments prepared in advance. These are very descriptively called "notice-and-comment" hearings because bureau officials are often doing no more than holding proceedings where affected parties are given a chance to respond only to what it is that the bureau wants to do.

In actual practice, neither form of pre-ruling public hearings is as rewarding or informative as theory would indicate. The regulations set through rule-making are all general ones applicable to broad categories of recipients. No specific judgments applicable to individual parties may be rendered nor may automatic sanctions be imposed on future violators.[5] And the interest groups most deeply involved in bureau affairs have been heard informally prior to the hearings. Therefore, since participatory incentives are small and because the most valued clients have already been involved, hearings mean little except to a few outside, "non-whirlpool" partners who have only a minimal chance of affecting major changes anyway. Other than that, hearings serve only to advance the cause of bureaus and their partners. Friendly congressmen, bureau officials, and interest group supporters use them to advertise the proposals they prefer and to demonstrate the strengths of their own preliminary planning development. In addition, hearings serve a symbolic purpose in that they add legitimacy to bureaucratic rule-making. The public nature of hearings gives organizations that are politically closed to external influence a contrary appearance of being open and broad-minded. Thus bureaucracy conforms to democratic expectations, a fact that promotes political stability and probably provides the greatest benefit that hearings offer as a result.

REGULATION, JUSTICE, AND THE COURTS

After general regulations have been established for the implementation of a bureau's legislative responsibilities, they still must be made applicable to specific situations before delivery can be made. Every year bureau officials interpret their regulations to make thousands of delivery-related decisions about who wins and who loses from publicly provided programs. Workman's compensation is approved for some and denied for others. A health care clinic is awarded to a San Francisco neighborhood while a similar application from Boston is turned down. One radio station has its license revoked and another has to revise its scheduling in order for its license to be renewed. Despite the great impact decisions like these have on those affected, they and most others are routine and will never be arbitrated by anyone outside the bureaucracy. Bureaus seldom need go to court to insure the enforcement of their regulations; and the incidence of appeals by aggrieved parties going to court is also very low.

Given the central position of the courts in most American contests over rights and justice, this is a unique situation. But, with regard to the precepts of administrative law, courts are to be avoided except in unusual situations. When regulatory decisions are contested, it is the bureaucracy rather than the court system that has original jurisdiction over conflicts between regulators and the regulated. If a bureau ruling is appealed, the plaintiff must begin the process at the bureau level. Then if the plaintiff decides to appeal further, the decision goes to hearing examiners within the independent agency or executive department. On the other hand, if the bureau wants to apply a general regulation to a specific corporation or individual, it can do so by ordering its representatives to appear at a bureau-initiated hearing. Should the defendant not comply with the decision, administrative officials can revoke licenses, withdraw funds, halt projects, or even levy a fine. Except for injunctions that temporarily suspend bureau rulings, the complaining bureau or regulated party will request a judicial trial only in the relatively infrequent instances when the defendant refuses to comply with the administrative decision. The limited intervention of the courts can be seen by contrasting the number of administrative trials to the number of cases heard by the courts during one year. In that period, nearly seventy thousand cases where heard by bureaucratic judges, while only a total of eleven thousand cases of *all* kinds, from individual felonies through regulatory appeals, were brought to the courts.[6]

The minimization of court interference in the regulatory process is the intent of those who promoted a viable and active bureaucracy.[7] Indeed independence from the courts was at the heart of the philosophy of those who felt bureaucracy was necessary to develop societal stability and fairness. Their logic was premised on the one resource that bureau officials have always used to secure influence—their expertise. It was felt from the middle of the nineteenth century on that only administrative tribunals could provide expert advice and intelligent overseers to decide on technical questions about such things as utilities, banking, commerce, and securities. Judges of the court, administrative theorists believed, lacked the necessary training, experience, and time to become adequately informed. In addition, they could never exercise continued oversight to ensure that orders were followed as could professional experts.

The relatively late emergence of public bureaucracy in the United States meant that concepts of administrative law were imposed upon a legal system that was already largely developed. Because administrative theorists had little faith in the ability of the courts, this situation produced the rather strange marriage of experts and jurists.

From the bureau's standpoint, adjustment to the resulting legal situation is not too difficult. In pursuing its desired programmatic ends, the bureau can always modify its demands and continue to seek compliance by prosecuting on the basis of the modified charges. In terms of obtaining justice and ultimately gaining freedom from external controls, the regulated rather than the bureaucratic regulators have the most complaints. After loosing in the courts, those being regulated must resign themselves to compliance rather than institute further legal action. The inability to question the substantive fairness and equity, or the justice, of bureaucratic regulations in the courts is the biggest disadvantage facing those regulated by government. For all practical purposes, they cannot do so. Those questions are left to the bureaucracy.

If the above sounds unreasonable, it is necessary to recall the importance expertise plays in recommending programs and successfully gaining legitimacy from those who voluntarily listen to bureau suggestions. As previously noted, the underlying legal philosophy of American bureaucracy emphasizes these same strengths. The concept of *judicial review*, which gives the courts the ability to determine whether a political decision is constitutional, has not been given much latitude to check bureau excesses in the area of administrative law. Bureau and court judges are to share the responsibility of ensuring administrative justice. And, according to this legal partnership, the courts are only to exercise authority after bureaucratic tribunals have acted on the specific merits of the plaintiff's case. Judicial review as it applies to bureaucracy is restricted to determinations about the statutory or constitutional authority of the rulings, proper interpretation of related regulations, procedural due process, and bureaucratic capriciousness. As a result, plaintiffs have no legal recourse before the courts when procedural hearing requirements are met and as long as the bureau has interpreted the enabling act as would some reasonable person.[8] Since reasonableness can be understood in innumerable ways, courts do not require that bureaus follow any definitions of what might be considered by another party as "the fairest or most efficient" means to the enabling legislation's end.[9] Quite specifically, "judicial review is not to insure the correctness of the administrative design."[10] To allow the courts the ability to intervene in substantive decisions would defeat the very purpose of bureaucracy.

As a result, however, private citizens have a very limited ability to challenge the goals of public programs and bureau actions designed to obtain them. When parties affected by a public program feel unfairly disadvantaged in its implementation, they can only go to the sponsoring bureau and register a protest. If, for instance, the Law Enforcement Assistance Administration turns down a grant application or cuts off funds to an ongoing project, the city's only formal opportunity to request a reconsideration is with LEAA. In the case of most grants and projects, this hearing will consist of little more than the bureau's explanation as to why the ruling was unfavorable. In these instances, there is no formal administrative trial or adjudication where the complainant can attempt to refute the bureau's charge in the presence of a judge or ruling board. Adjudications normally are only required for bureau decisions that directly apply government controls to completely private activities. For example, there must be a trial when there is conflict over licensing, rate hikes, or route changes determined by bureau regulations. Under their restrictions, the Federal Trade Commission cannot rule on whether an industrial firm has violated fair trade regulations until the firm can collect and present its evidence at a formal hearing. Nor can the Michigan DNR take final action to ban fishing for reasons of contamination without one or more administrative judges hearing the arguments of affected fishermen. However, after the judges decide, the regulated party's only option is to appeal to the courts on procedural grounds. Their ability to challenge the fairness or constitutionality of the specific action expires.

The separation between procedure and substance that separates administrative judgments from the authority of the court is theoretically justified on the basis of organizational safeguards. Those being regulated are supposed to be protected from arbitrary adjudication by the separation of administrative judges from the hierarchical structure of bureau officials who plan, prepare, and deliver programs. For instance, the Mining Enforcement and Safety Administration makes many rulings which impose restrictions on private parties such as coal mine operators. Usually these rulings follow inspections of operating facilities. When an inspector discerns a violation of the general regulations regarding safety standards, MESA officials can force compliance. But mine owners can appeal, demand adjudicatory hearings on the basis of their own evidence, and be given an opportunity to reverse the specific application of the MESA regulation. This will be administered through the Department of Interior's Office of Hearings and Appeals rather than MESA. Once this office has ruled, the decision is considered final by the department, and no staff or line level bureaucrat can alter it.

This type of organizational separation is the common form for most departments and agencies. If an agency has several bureaus enforcing private compliance with regulations, such a hearings office is almost certain to be present. Although officials within the appeals office specialize in order to retain the necessary expertise that distinguishes them from court judges, an autonomous office structure offers advantages in addition to just insulating trial personnel from the pressures of fellow bureau officials. It also allows continual information exchange and interaction among the specialists who need to develop a high level of competency in adjudicative procedure in addition to their substantive expertise. Also, a separate office allows the easy formation of ad hoc hearings and appeal boards when nonroutine disputes arise that do not fall within the categories of any established boards.

DOI's Office of Hearings and Appeals is a good example of an organization that allows judges to develop both procedural and substantive capabilities. In addition to the board responsible for MESA's mine health and safety concerns, there are other boards and individual judges specializing in Indian probate affairs, contract disputes, public lands and resources, submerged offshore lands, oil import quotas, and rare and endangered animal plant species.[11] In contrast to DOI, several smaller agencies like the Securities and Exchange Commission have some organizational difficulties because they must house their administrative judges within regular bureau structures. There is often no other alternative, since some agencies function as nothing more than single bureaus. But even in these situations, administrative law judges are given as much separate status as possible to ensure their independence of mind.

No matter how independent and professional administrative judges are, however, they can never be entirely removed from the organizational structure employing them. A great percentage, perhaps a majority, of judges are career bureaucrats without legal training; and even law school graduates normally work their way up through the bureau and agency hierarchy prior to assuming present positions. In doing so, there is no way for a jurist to avoid some organizational sympathies and loyalties. Such employees have been too identified with the various bureaus and their work to ever be completely unbiased in judging them. But there is little alternative to correct this problem. The situation will always exist as long as the doctrine of expertise is the guiding philosophy of administrative law.

Individuals do, of course, attempt to be impartial and fair. And almost no one argues that the organization of administrative justice is consciously stacked against those who are to be regulated in order to purposely disadvantage them. But it is clear that organizational loyalties, personal relationships, and job familiarities that come from regular working relationships, with fellow departmental and agency employees, and dedication to the role of government expert all combine to ally administrative judges with the goals of their own institution. Accordingly, both the general and specific rulings that govern implementation suffer from the same narrowness that characterize each of the three stages of the programmatic process.

THE PROBLEM OF COORDINATION

Since regulations are prepared and overseen by bureaucratic specialists, their net effect produces an uncoordinated system of legal obligations that no individual or institution can keep clear. As President Gerald Ford so aptly explained, American government has become a "mulligan stew of rules and regulations." Literally thousands of bureaus exist within the three levels of American government, and each of them sets some standards for those citizens under its jurisdiction. Probably no one will ever know how many benefits citizens are eligible for, or how many legal obligations they have, or how many administrative laws they mistakenly violate. In 1975 alone it took over forty-five thousand pages of the *Federal Register* just to list new regulations. Nor will anyone ever develop a clear model that explains what procedures bureaus must follow in establishing relationships with those they regulate. Bureaus do too much and are too unrestricted in the development of their own operational styles to act any other way.

The division of labor that results in thousands of autonomous bureaus makes it impossible for potential recipients and violators to be well informed until they come into direct contact with those who exert power over them. For many individuals and organizations, this information comes too late to obtain their rightful benefits or to avoid punishment. Although bureaus hold hearings, post and send notices, and even advertise through the mass media, great ignorance about the goods and services of government is the norm. It is too difficult for nonexperts to catch up and keep up with the vast number of programs that would affect them. The same is true of entire businesses and even other government organizations which might be subjected to the requirements of dozens of bureaus.

This complex situation shapes the way most modern organizations respond to government. To be sure, they seek demands and attempt reforms of government that are selectively rewarding to them. However, on a more regular basis, both private and public institutions employ "watchdog" lobbyists to scrutinize governmental outputs in order to keep abreast of new or modified regulations. Without such agents, those organizations might miss out on benefits, and their officials might openly but unwittingly violate the law. By hiring professional "watchdogs," organizations minimize such risks by attempting to avoid uncertainty about when and where government might intervene.

For similar kinds of reasons, governmental units and nonprofit associations increasingly employ professional grantsmen who systematically review available programs in order to determine whether or not other bureaus offer assistance to their problems and to find out what must be done to become eligible if that assistance exists. Also, industries and businesses hire specialists to learn about what kinds of projects bureaus might be funding. And these same individuals review and study volumes of regulations and daily government reports before embarking on any new venture. It is just as important for these private institutions to be able to accurately predict how government rules will affect profit and loss margins as it is to know what it is various bureaus will be purchasing. Private firms need, for instance, information about what conditions they must meet in selling their product to government: or they must understand how various regulations, such as those for environmental or consumer protection, either will add costs to corporate plans or deprive them of likely customers. Bureaucratic regulation makes it increasingly necessary for businesses to base expansion or marketing decisions on the impact regulations have on their internal operations. A brewery, for example, with a favorable contract from an aluminum can manufacturer might not find it profitable to expand into a likely state because that marketplace is restricted by requirements favoring producers using returnable bottles. In short, "watchdogs," grantsmen, and government analysts have constructed an indispensable, multi-billion-dollar enterprise for themselves on the basis of government's fragmented and extensive regulatory authority. Even though this enterprise works imperfectly, however, it is one that most citizens can neither afford nor effectively organize to duplicate.

POLITICAL RESPONSES TO REGULATION

Today American citizens seem to be upset about the regulatory power of bureaucracy. Does that mean profound changes are forthcoming that will limit the influence of bureaus? And, as a result, does it mean that there will be major changes in the way government makes its decisions about who gets what?

The simple fact that bureaucracy holds such a high potential for dominating the output of public programs makes it a likely issue for political controversy. One can easily imagine a society in revolt against bureaucracy because of great unhappiness with the allocation of government rewards and the number of sanctions and amount of costs that its members must pay. But, given citizen interest and unhappiness, is bureaucracy as a subject likely to emerge as a major political issue, or will it be a subject reduced merely to campaign rhetoric? And if bureaucracy does emerge as an issue, what aspects of it will be criticized and what related reforms will be proposed? The answers to these questions are not difficult to predict.

From all indications, regulatory powers will be the focus of any conflict. After all, the specific rulings that have an impact on citizens are felt, while most actions of bureaucrats have very limited visibility. Also, there is a general tendency for most casual observers, a description that clearly fits most voters, to focus primarily on the formal aspects of government. Given the limited knowledge citizens have about bureaucrats, it would be hard to envision an electorate informed and sophisticated enough to direct its discontent toward the informal influence of bureaucrats and the reliance on expertise that spawns it.

All our historical indicators confirm the belief that bureaucracy, if it becomes an issue, is attacked and defended on the basis of its regulatory role and little else. Even though political conflicts of the past never generated great concerns on the part of many citizens, the issue has always been aired essentially in regulatory terms. The 1970's has been no exception, even though politicians were not arguing the issue in the relative obscurity that surrounded past controversies. The period of the seventies appears to be one in which antibureaucratic sentiment increasingly developed as citizens responded to general campaign criticisms of "big government." President Ford's laments of 1975 were most illustrative of the prevailing political sentiment. "The federal government now employs over 100,000 people whose sole responsibility is the writing, reviewing, and enforcing of some type of regulation . . . One hundred thousand people whose principle job is telling you how to do your job. It's a bureaucrat's dream of heaven but it's a nightmare for those who have to bear the burden."

Even bureaucratic spokesmen for Ford dwelled on regulatory abuses linked to the theme of "too much government." The most emphatic remarks came from Health, Education and Welfare Secretary David Matthews as he publicly attacked the overly grand expectations of his departmental subordinates. Although his criticism was extensive, Dr. Matthews's most direct and most cogent remarks were toward the arrogance of HEW officials who found it necessary to intervene in clients' lives to the extent that they did such things as limit the number of days nursing home patients could spend away with friends or relatives during the Christmas season. In defending grandmother's right to another night on the town without loss of her government support, Matthews touched all the problems of regulatory coordination that have occasionally become political issues. Using grandparents as an object lesson, the secretary emphasized that: (1) government regulates too much, (2) it regulates the most defenseless more than the stronger, and, (3) regardless of personal or corporate strength, it exacts a great price from all regulated parties. Although the tone of voice and general emphasis varied, the same charges were made by nearly every one of the 1976 presidential candidates from liberal Birch Bayh through conservative Ronald Reagan.

Even though similar complaints have been aired before on the campaign trail and found sympathetic listeners, 1970 style rhetoric differed because electoral aspirants directed their arguments specifically against the overall regulatory pattern of bureaucratized government. Previously, those who made similar arguments were like Governor George Wallace, primarily interested in and aiming their attacks toward states' rights, business profits, or other more distinct issue areas. In terms of comparison, electoral politics in the seventies resembled only the few heightened controversies between presidents and legislators that occasionally surfaced at the federal level. These have been among the few other instances in recent American politics where more than a few dissidents challenged the general appropriateness of bureaucratic power.

When the issue of regulatory reform finds a place on the political agenda, it has usually been at the chief executive's urging. In fact, at the national level, where the greatest controversies have taken place, the emergence of the issue, with the exception of the first Hoover Commission, has been associated with the reports of presidential commissions. Since congressional interest in bureaucracy is more fragmented and piecemeal than the President's, his leadership should hardly be surprising. And, because of the President's many concerns and limited personal resources, it has always been impossible to develop a reform proposal without the assistance of an advisory group.

The first president to request a review of the bureaucracy was

Franklin D. Roosevelt, who commissioned a committee on administrative management with such participants as Louis Brownlow, Luther Gulick, and Lyndall Urwick. However, Roosevelt was more enamored by Gulick and Urwick's contention that they could develop internal principles for controlling the operation of bureaus and departments than he was cautious about regulatory authority.[12] The 1937 report of this Brownlow Committee detailed the need for developing a bureaucratic structure that centralized power and responsibility with the President.[13] Bureaucrats, the theme of the report urged, should have "passion for anonymity," and public management should be intended to assist them in becoming subservient to presidential preferences.

The Brownlow Committee report was a radical departure from the prevailing theory of bureaucracy that promoted independent regulation. According to Roosevelt's analysts, bureaucrats should listen to orders from above, pass information up for top-level political consideration, and generally remove themselves from actual rule-making. Moreover, they contended that bureaucrats had been too narrow, specialized, and technical in the past. What was needed, the report continued, were administrative generalists who could move decision-making up the hierarchy and out of the lower levels of bureaucracy by applying sound managerial techniques.

Although the legal status of the bureau's regulatory authority has never been weakened to meet the expectations of the Brownlow report, its themes of developing sound management principles and presidential authority have been central to each subsequent committee investigating bureaucratic reform. In fact, even the first Hoover Commission, which was Congress's response to the Brownlow report, and the many state-sponsored "little Hoover Commissions" did nothing more than extend the Brownlow arguments. Even the very technically advanced Planning, Programming, and Budgeting System as it was formulated in the 1960's and extended under President Johnson's executive order was nothing more than continued elaboration upon the Brownlow recommendation that the Bureau of the Budget be used as a management tool to facilitate presidential control of bureaucracy.

A review of the recommendations of the first Hoover Commission illustrates, in part, why these original commissions never undermined the legal powers of bureaucracy. The question was never really confronted, even though regulation was the central concern. Hoover report topics included unity in administration, presidential-legislative involvement with policy-level bureaucrats, civil service, category routings for testing, purchasing, points of organization confusion, standardized terminology, budgeting, apportionment of funds, and fund reductions. Instead of questioning the application of regulatory power, the commission spent its time tinkering with management techniques to improve central control. Even when specific policy areas and the substance of regulation were specifically considered, the emphasis of the report was on bringing rule-making to the top of the organization's hierarchy and away from the discretionary responses of subordinates.

The neglect of specifically regulatory reforms by the commissions reporting prior to 1955 only partially accounts for government's inability to grapple with what was considered the real problem even though general support existed for the greater involvement of elected representatives in the regulatory process. The second Hoover Commission, which reported to President Eisenhower, and President Nixon's Ash Council both deviated from other commissions and recommended substantial changes in regulatory power. Hoover II's recommendations called for stripping away much of the quasi-judicial role of bureaucracy and reassigning it to the courts, more extensive judicial review, greater independence for administrative judges, and total separation between the investigative and adjudicatory work of bureaus. In a word, the proposed reforms were radical alterations in regulatory theory.

What were the results of this great confrontation? Was there a reconciliation between the theory of administrative law and the desire for politically responsible bureaucracy? No! None of the proposals were adopted. In fact, the second Hoover Commission had almost no impact, general or specific, on the regulatory authority of bureaucracy. Why? In part, the second commission went further than political sentiment allowed. Congress made it clear that its concerns with regulation, as expressed in the request for the first Hoover Commission, extended only to the responsiveness of bureaucracy to elected politicians. Few legislators could accept the idea of weakening bureaus and strengthening the courts' position. In addition, the second Hoover Commission generated little support because its advocates were mostly staff and members of the American Bar Association. Even Hoover Commission staff members hotly disagreed over the appropriateness of the recommendations. In the end, because of the obvious interest of the Bar Association in increasing court litigations, not even Eisenhower would strongly endorse the recommendations for removing regulatory autonomy from the bureaucracy.

However, the second Hoover report also failed because it potentially disrupted Congress's domain. Bureaus that responded to the requests of individual legislators would be deprived of much of their ability to achieve desired programmatic goals; and, as a result, congressmen who were able to gain individual satisfactions from bureau activities would also lose. In short, by rejecting the second Hoover report, Congress voted to maintain its own political prominence just as an earlier Congress had done in refusing to go along with more than a handful of agency reorganization proposals outlined in the first report. Later Congress was to do the same thing when it refused to give a recently elected President Nixon any support in advancing his major bureaucratic reorganization plan. And it did the same to the Ash Council's rather moderate proposals that came later. Congress could not accept any reorganizing of the structural arrangements of regulatory bureaus; and legislators similarly cold-shouldered all proposals that were designed to change administrative procedures in order to minimize "overjudicialization."

In the final analysis, political controversy over bureaucracy has been little more than a struggle between two branches of government vying with one another for power. Presidents have wanted more influence over rules and regulation, and congressmen have not wished to lose their own. But neither party has worried much about the regulatory problems of the citizenry. "Vested interest," more than any other factor, accounts for the continued regulatory autonomy of bureaucracy. When the bureau's power to control others is threatened, its congressional supporters are threatened. And they have always reacted as one would expect, protecting their partner institutions. For the same reason presidents have always been interested in moving regulatory authority to the top of the hierarchy, not to the courts.

Will things change, with presidents and presidential candidates finding the electoral arenas a congenial place for extending their criticisms of bureaucracy? Will the regulatory issue bring about reform because of voter involvement in the matter? Will public sentiment outweigh a legislator's commitment to bureaucratic supporters? Or will the two factors even come into conflict once the election has passed? While there are no obvious answers to these questions, most of them have been suggested throughout this book, and it appears that there is very little prospect for change. President Ford's campaign against what he charged to be "regulatory abuses" also provides some insight into the reasons why not.

Ford began his antibureaucratic, anti-"big government" campaign soon after assuming office from resigning President Nixon. Among his criticisms, the President addressed social programs that bureaus "couldn't make work," the improper regulation of airlines and railroads, and burdensome restrictions that all citizens face. While doing so, he called for high-level conferences to systematically and comprehensively deal with regulatory reform. The conferences began in June 1975. First, the President met with twenty-four leaders of the House and Senate while his staff members met with counsels representing the independent regulatory agencies. Then a bureaucratic summit meeting brought President Ford and the members of ten regulating bureaus together. From all outward appearances, a major White House effort was being carried out.

But then the activity ended. All that remained was Ford's rather abstract nonspecific campaign rhetoric in which he promised to resolve the whole question by appointing a third Hoover Commission sometime after the 1976 election. With regard to daily bureaucratic activities, the only agreements that the President forced were ones to cut down burden- some paperwork, to lessen the costs of bureau operations, and to take in- flationary factors into greater account in making rulings. No specific programs were cut, no massive layoffs were proposed, and none of either were promised. In fact, some bureaus like the Council on Wage and Price Stability were quietly extending their regulatory authority at the height of Ford's criticism. Even the President was simultaneously discussing the need for new regulations to protect health and safety. Nothing that was happening indicated that President Ford was about to challenge the foundation of public bureaucracy on behalf of the American citizenry.

More probably, the President had already accomplished his primary goals. He had effectively gained public support by identifying with an attractive issue, one modifying what George Wallace had capitalized on so well in 1972, and one that Ford did not want co-opted entirely by Jimmy Carter and Ronald Reagan in 1976. At the same time, the President made it clear to bureau officials that they were working in an austere period and they should readjust accordingly. If he were to pursue the matter further, however, there would be a decided risk. Accelerated attacks would have to be directed toward specific programs and that would mean that a confrontation would be automatically forthcoming were he to be reelected. As with all other electoral issues, an abstract antibureaucratic campaign is by no means a perfect indicator of further governmental trends. It wins no guaranteed future supporters, since specific questions about who will gain and lose are undefined. Nor does it determine for the President whether it is worthwhile to promote a reorganization proposal. In the final analysis, that depends on whether the bureaucracy is satisfying the President's leadership needs with regard to controlling public programs. And that determination can be, indeed usually is, very far removed from electoral politics. At least it was very clear in the election and campaign of 1976 that there would never be a specific reform proposal advanced to gain electoral support. Nor would citizens demand one. If the election inspired continued discussion of bureaucratic reform as promised by Ford's third Hoover Commission, it did so by removing the issue of bureaucracy from the arena of citizen politics and back into the age old clandestine struggle between the executive and legislature.

SUMMARY

Among the rules of bureaucracy, there exists "regulation." The enabling acts that come from the legislature seldom contain all the provisions necessary to deliver public goods and services. So the bureaucracy is delegated the responsibility of arranging the means to achieve programmatic ends. The interpretive power of bureaus leaves them the right to set procedures and limit the actions of those touching or touched by public programs. Since government decided to undertake massive programmatic action to contribute positively to the general well-being of the citizenry, regulation has become an essential part of bureaucracy.

As bureaucratic regulation has increased, an elaborate quasi-judicial process of hearings and judges has been established as well. But this process neither produces many changes in public programs nor keeps potentially affected citizens especially aware of government requirements. As a result, bureau regulations and the limits they impose on all of our lives have become the sources of great frustration to many Americans.

Not unexpectedly, these frustrations have been translated into political issues and campaigns. The 1976 presidential election, in particular, promised to focus on bureaucratic excess in regulation. However, the conflict that many expected never materialized as much more than a symbolic gesture. Elected politicians, as in the past, found it extremely difficult to wage a concentrated war against their bureaucratic allies. And the citizenry, also dependent on public services, found it equally impossible to direct its anger against faceless officials in invisible, little-understood bureaus.

SECTION FOUR

POLITICAL CHANGE
AND THE BUREAUCRACY

8...

BUREAUCRACY THREATENED—
the POLITICS of the 1970's

Politics, 1970 style, has been full of antibureaucratic sentiment. And, while what transpired has been reminiscent of the empty threats of earlier times, most administrators experienced many an uneasy moment whenever they pondered their future. After reading news analyses and listening to television reports, bureaucrats found it easy to temporarily forget how well entrenched and needed their programs and bureaus have become. Instead these officials often fearfully wondered if there is a place for them in a world where voters, presidents, and even other bureaucrats appear to be out to terminate their influence. As understandable as they are, these fears proved largely unfounded. The major threats to bureaucracy in the seventies had little impact and produced few dramatic changes. The most significant changes have come about as bureaus themselves have adapted to changing conditions.

THE 1976 ELECTION

Since presidential elections are the major political events for the media and public, the 1976 campaign might well have caused bureaucrats the greatest discomfort. The Wallace-Carter-Ford denunciations of big government and regulation were repeated almost daily while the candidates were moving to center stage for the election.[1] And the campaigners were all portrayed by the *Washington Post* and CBS as near-zealots in their opposition to bureaucratized government. By early 1975, anyone who accepted campaign speechs at anything near face value must have believed that bureaucrats were in big trouble. Then candidate Jimmy Carter declared:

"Our government in Washington now is a horrible bureaucratic mess." "It is," he added, "disorganized, wasteful, has no purpose; and its policies—when they exist—are incomprehensible or devised by special interest groups with little regard for the welfare of the average American citizen."

The public too was unsympathetic to bureaucrats. Not long after the election, opinion pollsters found that large numbers of Americans felt that there were too many bureaucrats in government and that those employees received too much money for too little work. According to George Gallup, over two-third of the public exhibited such feelings.[2]

Yet, after all the commentary, nothing of any great consequence came of the election. Proposals for bureaucratic reorganization, projected areas for deregulation, plans for scaling down bureaucracy; all of these were, for the most part, conspicuously absent from the campaign. Indeed, by campaign's end in September and October, the candidates were backing off on the entire issue of bureaucracy. When the subject was brought up at all, it was in response to outside questions rather than in the form of new ideas among the candidates' prepared remarks.

In short, the presidential election of 1976 left no specific threat to bureaucracy, no assembled blueprints for change. Contrary to what many observers might have expected, 1976 was not the culmination of a trend set in general motion in earlier elections. It was not the year the citizenry was given a grand and detailed plan for bureaucratic reform. There was little explicitly promised that President Carter had to follow through on for particular departments or agencies after the inauguration.

And it was apparent by election time that no grand plan was in demand by the voters. The major issues of the campaign were the economy and employment.[3] The 1973-1974 recession had left a deep mark on the personal well-being and purchasing power of most Americans, and they could feel that impact very directly. Bureaucracy was of interest only in that citizens wanted a government that operated effectively to solve their economic problems and, to a much lesser extent, efficiently without great financial waste. It was to this point, and only to this point, that Ford and Carter turned when they addressed bureaucracy during the final weeks of the campaign.

The social issues of race and busing and moral issues like abortion were also of more critical concern to the electorate than bureaucracy.[4] The more they emerged as such, the more it became apparent that who-ever captured the election would depend on the bureaucracy for his solutions. Bureaus would have to deliver Carter's more equitable and stable welfare program or police Ford's attack on "welfare cheats." In other issue areas, it became clear that the candidates were addressing problems that involved bureaucracy in cleaning up its own house and improving its operation. Organizations like the Bureau of Mines were to expand and hasten the development of coal technology. The Central Intelligence Agency was to fine-tune its information-gathering capabilities and improve its liaison with the White House and Congress. And, as Jimmy Carter saw it, the many bureaus of the foreign policy network would have to step forward and contribute more to a team effort in international affairs. By directly attacking Henry Kissinger as the "Lone Ranger" of foreign policy, Carter was calling for the other experts in the Defense and State departments to come forward and perform up to their levels of ability.

This same tendency to increase bureaucratic involvement and programmatic support was also apparent in Carter's appeal to special interests. For example, one of candidate Carter's most specific statements was his support for a new Department of Education.[5] In addressing the National Education Association during the summer of 1976, Carter declared his support for this new Cabinet-level status because he saw it providing a "stronger voice for education." This address, as well as others like it, were more statements of pro-bureaucratic sympathy than anything else; if carried to their logical conclusion, they meant more bureaucracy rather than less.

Apart from the low priority of the bureaucracy as an issue is the fact that issues alone appeared to be of little importance to the outcome of the 1976 presidential election. Election analysis showed that the vote was primarily a party one supplemented by an ideological split.[6] That is, four out of five Democrats voted for Carter and nine out of ten Republicans voted for Ford. In addition, Carter drew 75 percent of the liberal votes, while Ford gained support from 70 percent of the conservatives. At the end of the long campaign, it was these factors and Carter's "new political face" that determined the outcome.[7] No issue, especially the demise of bureaucracy, had turned the voters on and led them to clamor for action on behalf of campaign promises.

One question remains from the presidential election of 1976, however. Why, in the midst of so much antibureaucratic rhetoric, did the issue matter so little in the election? Voters, electoral analysis shows, plainly did not care very much. So the answer seems to lie in the candidates, and the media as well. The candidates quite obviously attempted to capitalize on George Wallace's early appeal. But the candidates of 1976 never fully realized that Wallace's appeal was in his total appearance of disdain for conventional establishment ways.[8] Wallace was not just a new face who was anti-"big government" or antiregulation. George Wallace represented complete opposition to what was fashionable in government, and he represented that outlook to supporters who were very disenchanted with government.

The candidates of 1976 could not pick up only a portion of the Wallace image and effectively attract supporters. They tried and failed. However, the candidates succeeded in capturing the fancy of the mass media with their antibureaucratic statements. And, because media coverage was so intense and so concerned about detailed opinions of the candidates, it appears as if the media kept the issue alive throughout the campaign.[9] Bureaucracy, it would seem, was an issue which moved politically aware and knowledgeable journalists but not the public. While the electorate was apparently willing to listen to and even eagerly accept antibureaucratic comments from the candidates, that citizenry could not see bureaucratic action as directly affecting their lives. As an issue, bureaucracy was too abstract to be long-lived or given a high voter priority.

CARTER'S REORGANIZATION

Even though the voters did not demand it, President Carter was forced to address administrative reorganization early in his first term. His credibility and personal preferences made action mandatory. However, what the President thought would be early and quick attention came to be a continued and ongoing interest.

To reorganize, the new President and his personal staff first had to determine the logistics of how to proceed. Presidential resources are extremely limited when it comes to firing personnel, eliminating programs, or consolidating bureaus. Even simple shifts of manpower, activities, and bureaus are generally beyond his authority. Although precedents had established the President's right to undertake limited reorganizations on his own in times of war or other national emergencies, it was clear to all political participants that the Congress would never allow Carter to reorder the bureaucracy through executive order, accept for his own personal offices.

There were, therefore, only three other options open to Carter.[10] One, he could request Cabinet members to undertake minimal reorganization independently within their own departments. Or, two and three, he could work with the Congress to change the bureaucracy either through legal statute or a formal reorganization plan.

The first option was of limited assistance to the President's desire for autonomous action, since, over the years, Congress has increasingly been prone to intervene if its members opposed proposed changes. As a result, Carter's hopes for a reorganized bureaucracy clearly rested on congressional assistance whichever option or combination of options he pursued. To maximize its effectiveness, the White House elected to reorganize using all of the possible methods, including some executive orders, depending on whichever one was most appropriate to the bureaus and programs under consideration at any one time.

Congress entered into the President's strategy yet another way. In this case, Congress was important since it had a hand in a multiplicity of concerns other than reorganization which demanded the immediate attention of the new administration. During his first year in office, Carter and his staff had to give their attention to an incredible number of priorities. Energy legislation, the SALT agreement with the Soviet Union, a treaty on the Panama Canal, peace talks in the Middle East, welfare reform, and a social security revision all had to be pushed; none could be given a back seat, because they were all issues judged to be critical to the administration. To succeed at all, Carter had to have legislative support behind every issue. Support, however, was not obviously present or easily won, and inexperienced White House personnel had their hands full with this huge bundle of demands they were making on Congress. Not only were the Carter people too busy to promote reorganization, it was also necessary to push it slowly because of the likelihood for conflict. Reorganization, Carter acknowledged, would be full of controversies, and the need to mend legislative fences on these other issues made it an inopportune time to push many bureaucratic changes and make additional enemies.

In addition to congressional relations, there were also the questions of what to reorganize and who should be affected. The size and complexity of the bureaucracy coupled with Carter's status as a first term, and therefore inexpert, "Washington insider" meant that information about "what" and "who" was particularly difficult to come by. White House staffers were also new to Washington and were busy with other priorities anyway. The Congress, of course, was an impossible source since fragmented influence within the legislature rested on bureau support. These subgovernments of bureaucrats and legislators, or the "whirlpools of activity" cited in Chapter 3, had never shown an inclination to reform operations from within. Therefore, the White House had to rely on its own people and their allies for reorganization planning. It chose the Office of Management and Budget.

In 1977, the Reorganization Project, a bureau within OMB, was assigned primary responsibility for developing reorganization plans. That unit's job is to identify areas of needed change, pinpoint problems, and propose corrective action. Because it has limited manpower and budget, the Reorganization Project cannot review every bureau and program in turn. Instead it must proceed piecemeal to identify the most pressing problem areas. By late 1977, the project was sponsoring some thirty studies in such diverse areas as border law enforcement, disaster preparedness, and food and nutrition policy.[11]

White House reliance on OMB contributed to the slow-paced, piecemeal approach to reorganization that congressional relations and other priorities had already forced on the Carter administration. The Reorganization Project was not only absolutely small, it was also only one small portion of the whole Office of Management and Budget. And OMB in the past has shown a decided reluctance to interfere with the internal operation of other bureaus during reorganizing because of its need to continue working with them on budget matters.[12] As a control agency, OMB needs good working relations with those it must supervise; and an investigation relative to reorganization constitutes a threat to those relationships. So some timidity was found within OMB; and this timidity increased when OMB director and chief Carter confidant Bert Lance was forced to leave government due to his banking irregularities.

Jimmy Carter's own promises also added to the slowness of reorganization since he seriously constrained the kinds of proposals that could be entertained.[13] In addressing the bureaucracy, Carter committed himself to reorganization plans that would be worked through with the involvement of the bureaus to be affected. Therefore, bureaus and their supervisory departments and agencies can and do gear up to defend themselves and often even call in their outside subgovernment allies for support.

The President further promised that no one would be fired or reduced in rank as a result of reorganization. If jobs were to be eliminated, normal attrition through retirements and job transfers would have to handle all cuts. In other words, Carter set one important guideline for those assisting him with reorganization—no huge cuts or dramatic program shifts.

With such difficulties and constraints, bureaucratic reorganization, if it were to occur, would be undramatic. The gradual changes within the Carter administration have indeed proven to be colorless and without great threat to bureau or "whirlpool" influence. However, there have been interesting changes which mirror the current issues confronting American government during the late 1970's. In this respect, reorganization has been significant because it demonstrates the political responsiveness of a president interested in the impact of bureaucracy upon society.

The First Phase of Reorganization. In order to maximize the number of options open to the President in reorganizing, Carter, in early February of his first year in office, requested the Congress to reactivate the expired Reorganization Act of 1949. Under that act, the President could submit individual nonamendable plans for the reorganization of logically consistent subjects to the Congress. If the Congress did not vote, by simple majority rule, to override the President within sixty calendar days of continuous congressional session, the reorganization plan being proposed was to go into effect. With the passage of the Reorganization Act, the President was given the flexibility to reorganize without resorting to statute. That is, under the Reorganization Act of 1977, Carter could reorganize segments of the bureaucracy without a vote in Congress. Without the act, he would have been forced to reorganize within departments or by submitting to the Congress individual bills for every proposed change in present laws. Since that latter option would have meant the cumbersome involvement of several committees and the endless possibility of amendments, the 1977 act's approval provided ease and flexibility to Mr. Carter's hopes, at least for the three years that the bill was to be in effect.

Even with the Reorganization Act, White House capability is limited. Since the plans must be limited to single subjects such as food policy or the justice system, large segments of the bureaucracy cannot be reorganized at one time. The President also is restricted by the number of bills that the Congress can consider at any one time, three. In that way, Mr. Carter is unable to follow a strategy of forcing no legislative response by burying or overburdening Congress with bureaucratic matters. Provisions of the act also prevent the President from arranging to lock plans up in committees without adequate time for consideration by the whole House or Senate. Thus, while offering the President the opportunity to reorganize at his own discretion, the Congress put him on notice that legislative involvement was to be expected.

Reorganizing the Executive Office. The first official Reorganization Plan within the Carter Administration was a proposal submitted in July 1977 to eliminate seven of the units of the Executive Office and create one replacement. Abolished were the Council on International Economic Policy, Office of Telecommunications Policy, Federal Property Council, Office of Drug Abuse Policy, Energy Resources Council, and Economic Opportunity Council. The Domestic Policy Staff was established and the Domestic Council cut. These proposals followed the previous executive order to end the operation of two presidential advisory bodies, the Economic Policy Board and the President's Foreign Intelligence Advisory Board.[14] Coinciding with the plan, Carter ordered a cutback in White House Office staff from 485 to 351.

There were several reasons why reorganization started in the President's own bureaucracy. Perhaps most important was the political controversy the swelling size of the Executive Office generated. Only two months after Carter took office, 30 percent more staff personnel were working in the White House than ever before. Since Carter had, during the campaign, talked of a bloated Republican presidential staff, the growth under his new administration had to be more than a little embarrasing. However, the ease of reorganizing those units closest to the President and the need to get his own operation finally under way also contributed to the decision. But not the least important reason was the symbolic value of starting transfers and cuts close to home. If the President expected bureaucratic and popular support for his reorganization efforts, it was necessary to set a sound, even sacrificial, example for those bureaucrats who would have to undergo the later traumas of change.

Establishing an Energy Department. The most consequential bureaucratic reordering of the early Carter administration was the creation of a federal Department of Energy in August 1977. At that time, the President signed into law a statute establishing the twelfth Cabinet-level department. Because of the complexity of the changes, and because the proposal originated prior to the Reorganization Act of 1977, the creation of this department necessitated active legislative involvement, and the President's plan was substantially altered by Congress.

The resulting Department of Energy brought together the diverse energy agencies of the federal government including the Federal Energy Administration and the Energy Research and Development Administration. It also took over most of the energy-related activities of the Department of the Interior and other agencies whose work dealt with energy development, conservation, and availability. Regulatory controls, beyond the normal authority of other departments, were built into DOE as it also assumed the previous powers of the Federal Power Commission. With the elimination of FPC, a five-member Federal Energy Regulatory Commission was set up to license and set rates for energy services. Although part of the department, FERC rulings are not subject to review outside the commission in the secretary's office.

The significance of DOE's creation was threefold. First, the administration addressed reorganization in the context of an issue which was creating tremendous social and economic problems. Thus, it proved its responsiveness and attentiveness while demonstrating that reorganization was not just empty rhetoric. Second, previously fragmented bureaus were drawn together for the first time, allowing for the possibility of comprehensive planning. Overnight twenty thousand federal employees had a common set of guidelines. Before, not even a general outline existed for bringing about a shared energy purpose. Finally, a focal point for formulating energy policy and bringing together energy interests was created. If nothing else, all the participants in energy policy knew exactly where to go to press their demands. The kind of shopping around for the best bargain that various interests engaged in prior to DOE's creation is no longer as feasible since former FEA, ERDA, FPC, and Interior officials now have less ability to go their own ways.

Internal Reorganization. Despite the importance of DOE's creation, reorganization during the first year of the Carter administration made more actual changes within ongoing departments. Health, Education and Welfare, Housing and Urban Development, and Agriculture all took the initiative and reorganized on their own under the supervision of their departmental secretaries. HEW, in fact, reacted so quickly to the President's call that the department was chastized by the Office of Management and Budget because OMB was not apprised of the changes before they happened.

Neither these early actions nor the reaction of OMB were suprising. All three departments were beset by major problems; and the call for reorganization served as an excuse for forcibly dealing with whatever plagued them. HEW made most of its internal moves to handle the problems of welfare, health care, and student loan fraud and abuse. A Health Care Financing Administration and a Bureau of Student Financial Assistance were both created, while multiple social service functions were divided up between the existent Social Security Administration and the Office of Human Development.

The primary conflicts in HUD had long centered around regional office autonomy. Therefore, when reorganization occurred, the power of those offices was downgraded and efforts were taken to purge them by moving their personnel. At USDA, a gigantic department with one bureaucrat for every thirty-four American farmers and an operation sorely in need of more clients, reorganization was aimed at providing greater responsiveness to consumers and nonfarm rural residents.

Internal reorganization made it strategically more plausible for departments to resist future changes that might not be so much in keeping with general departmental needs. When major changes have just occurred, it becomes more difficult for a president to disrupt things again. For those areas of HEW, HUD, and USDA that have been renovated, the chances are greater that the departments will continue their control. In areas not yet subjected to change, presidential intervention is more likely. However, because departments have emphasized changes in their biggest trouble spots, they have generally minimized the prospects for presidential intervention.

Strategy of this sort is consistent with the defensive stance normally taken by departmental heads; and it makes clear the fact that the departments are not the property of the White House. HEW Secretary Joseph Califano, one of the reorganizers, once observed that Cabinet officers destined to lose programs during reorganization traditionally oppose the plans.[15] As 1977 concluded, Agriculture Secretary Bob Bergland, another internal reorganizer, went on record saying he was prepared to fight should OMB suggest the transfer of any of his department's agencies. History, recent events, and comments of this kind suggest the likelihood of a continued emphasis on internal reorganization within departments and independent agencies. Of course, this means that Carter's reorganization will not truly be the President's.

Other changes. By 1978, a pattern had been established for reorganization of the Carter bureaucracy. Most of the actual reorganization would be internal; but to conform to the watchdog eye of Congress it could not be overly extensive; and interested legislators would be consulted by departmental and agency reorganizers. As with HEW, HUD, USDA, reorganization would deal with the most pressing and visible problems of the organizations as a whole.

Additional reorganization under the 1977 act would generally target in on extremely fragmented activities that were less than the primary functions of the department or agency. This minimizes threats to bureaucrats, legislators, and involved interest groups. Indirectly, as a result, it minimizes the President's chances of making enemies. The Second Reorganization Plan, which created the Agency for International Communication, provided a successful model for such change. In establishing AIC, communications programs of the U.S. Information Agency and the Bureau of Educational and Cultural Affairs were combined. Since neither unit was eliminated, the transformation was relatively noncontroversial. After a smooth transfer, similar recommendations followed from OMB for statistical organizations and border control.

Massive departmental shifts were to be avoided, with but a few necessary exceptions. After Interior lost much of its status and operations to the new Energy Department, much of its reason for existence had been eliminated. So efforts had to be made to change that department's mandate to one of primarily environmental purpose. Also, because of intense but divided educational lobbying, the creation of a Department of Education apart from HEW had to be considered. President Carter's campaign promises made that an essential matter; and congressional supporters of the plan had proposed its statutory creation already in 1977. Despite these conditions, opposition to such a proposal was strong, and it passed only narrowly in the fall of 1979.

Congress and the President. At each step, congressional opponents of the President generated considerable opposition. Mr. Carter did not get the Reorganization Act he wanted or the Energy Department he preferred. Both were attacked, held up, and amended. Nor did Carter escape criticism in other proposals. Although he succeeded, the elimination of the Office of Drug Abuse Policy and the creation of the Agency for International Communication were challenged even though one was in his own office and another a relatively minor change.

Congress, in all these transactions, was not a friendly arena for the new President even though he enjoyed certain advantages. Democrats in Congress wanted to assist him where possible. As a new President, he was enjoying his honeymoon period. A belief that some reorganization was needed existed throughout Congress. With regard to the Department of Energy, it was a critical issue demanding urgent attention. Finally, congressional allies such as Senator Abraham Ribicoff (D.-N.Y.) consistently intervened on the President's behalf.

Given what Mr. Carter obtained in 1977, and keeping those favorable conditions in mind, the critical importance of Congress loomed as a large hurdle for continued reorganization. Some easy matters still remained. But with more controversial matters under consideration by the Reorganization Project, 1978 and beyond appeared full of hard knocks. As Mr. Califano of HEW once forecast, "a president can at best achieve one or two major reorganizations during his years in office—if he selects his targets shrewdly."[16] Mr. Carter, for the remainder of his presidency, lived under that ominous prediction.

SETTING NEW AGENDAS

Although future reorganizations pose little if any threat to bureaucratic operations as we have known them, another type of challenge is now on the scene, presenting greater likelihood of forced change. That more ominous challenge is to the control of the bureau's internal agenda. As a result of its presence, many bureaus might find themselves emphasizing different programs, projects, and operational techniques than their officials would otherwise prefer.

Every organization and deliberative body lists those items and issues that must be considered and investigated for possible action. Such a list is known as the official agenda; and items on it are given at least approximate priority status. That is, items are listed in terms of their general importance to the organization because everything cannot be dealt with at once. And many things have to be postponed indefinitely.[17] The public bureaucracy is no exception. Departments, agencies, and bureaus all prepare their own agendas as part of their problem-solving, program development work.

Traditionally, bureaus have derived their political strength as government's resident experts from the fact that they have at least helped set their own agendas. Oftentimes they have completely dominated agenda setting. For example, the Law Enforcement Assistance Administration has been able to set priority projects for funding with little intervention from the White House or Congress. LEAA officials had only to worry about pleasing units of government who receive their grants and other attentive parties in the law enforcement field when those were the only items on their agenda which demanded attention. Similarly most bureaus within the United States Department of Agriculture have been able to fill their agendas with price supports, loans and credit, farm services, research, and educationally related projects because those were the ones valued by the rest of the agricultural establishment: congressional committees, farm interest groups, large-scale farmers, land grant colleges, and state departments of agriculture. By being involved at this level in the policy process, bureaus have been able to seize the initiative on program direction and bend it to best suit their own needs and capabilities.

But, to an important degree, this situation is gradually changing. With increasing frequency, bureaucrats are finding their own agendas clogged with items originating outside the organization and reflecting the program interest of others. Don Paarlberg, former Director of Agricultural Economics with the U.S. Department of Agriculture, claims to have been suddenly startled by the impact of a formal agenda of pressing USDA issues which was forwarded to him. Of all the items on that agenda, not one related to increasing productivity, maintaining farm incomes, sponsoring agricultural research, or any of the other programs continuously advocated by USDA since the depression of the 1930's. In their place were demands to hold down food prices, provide more food programs to the poor, answer environmental questions about fertilizers and pesticides, as well as serve nonfarm rural development interests. USDA was also being asked to deal with land use questions, civil rights, and collective bargaining as these issue areas merged with agricultural production.[18]

Moreover, these demands and requests did not come from a bureau's old congressional allies or interest group partners. Nor were they sent spiraling downward through the USDA bureaucratic hierarchy. "New agenda" items for agriculture and elsewhere are coming from sources unfamiliar to the bureaucrats who must handle them.[19] Consequently, these officials find themselves on uncertain, unsteady ground as they seek to become familiar enough with these new parties to begin the process of political bargaining. Not unexpectedly, they proceed with caution, reserve, skepticism, and frequently even resentment as these intruders are confronted.

Issues that come before bureaus on their new agendas appear to have two primary sources. One source includes organized groups and other interests whose demands have received public and, oftentimes, media attention. The second is comprised of other bureaus simply exercising responsibility over programs within their assigned jurisdictions. In some issue areas, bureaus receive similar and even combined pressure from both sources.

A large number of interests with varied political backgrounds now engage bureaus that have previously dealt with a more limited range of clientele.[20] Some of these interests, like the consumer movement spearheaded by the Consumer Federation of America, have only recently emerged and organized into political forces. They are now addressing bureaucrats in, among other places, the Departments of Agriculture, Commerce, and Transportation. Others such as the several groups that make up the poor people's hunger lobby, have been active in politics for a long period of time but are now moving in on new targets. Previously these organizations had lobbied on behalf of public housing and direct welfare payments; but in the past few years they have extended their efforts toward the influencing of those bureaucrats responsible for food stamps—that is, officials from the U.S. Department of Agriculture's Food and Nutrition Service.

Interest groups that have not assumed client status have a great deal of difficulty getting their issues on a bureau's agenda. They lack a track record of previous influence and, therefore, have neither the routine attention of the bureaucrats nor automatic access to them. So they normally resort to some extraordinary measure to gain attention and open doors. Consumers, for example, were quite successful with USDA when they held a national food boycott. Farm laborers and their supporters tried to accomplish the same agenda consideration by promoting grape, wine, and lettuce boycotts on behalf of collective bargaining rights.

If bureaucrats fail to give a hearing to the demands of those promoting new agenda items, they appear unresponsive and aloof to whoever observes their action. For most bureaus and their officials, such an image is damaging because it reflects negatively on legislative allies and the entire administration. In other words, it can cost vital political support. So bureaucrats listen when these extraordinary actions by outside interest groups begin to get attention.[21] And the more attention the groups get, the more consideration they receive. For that reason, interests representing issues having a large public following are more likely to gain places on new agendas. These issues—which include the environment, labor, civil rights, human needs, consumerism, public safety, and governmental corruption— are furthered in their pursuit of agenda status by the fact that the mass media provides them coverage because they attract public interest.

The second source of demand for new agenda items is the rest of the bureaucracy. As noted in Chapter 4, bureaus must often work either with one another or with one another's regulations. Most of the new agenda items which trouble bureau officials are not cooperative interbureau programs—at least not as yet. The troublesome ones are the programs designed to accomplish their goals through regulatory means when the regulated parties include other public bureaus. In this respect, bureau officials are not unlike other citizens who express resentment toward the regulatory process.

Examples of such regulatory programs imposed on bureaus include Affirmative Action and Equal Employment Opportunity, energy conservation, unionization rights within the organization, environmental impact statements, occupation safety, freedom of information, and the operation of government in the "sunshine." All bureaus must conform to related regulations before they can proceed with their own program responsibilities. In addition, a number of bureaus must contend with selected other regulatory programs in developing and implementing their plans. Agricultural bureaus, for instance, must not violate pesticide regulations from the Environmental Protection Agency, food additive rulings from the Food and Drug Administration, and foreign policy trade restrictions of the State Department. With such a myriad of bureaus to contend with before work could begin on matters of his own concern, it becomes easy to appreciate Director Paarlberg's fear that "the agricultural establishment has, in large measure, lost control of the agricultural policy agenda."[22]

The tasks confronting bureaucracy in dealing with the new agendas they face are difficult and tedious. In some cases, items can be considered, rejected, and removed from the agenda without action. But in a great many more instances, that alternative is impossible. Some groups will be impossible to put off because of the degree of their political support. And most of the regulations facing bureaucracy cannot be avoided. As noted above, they must be brought into the process of developing programs.

As a result, program operations and even the bureau's actual programs may change considerably. For example, bureaus within the Department of Defense had to adjust their internal operations by an estimated $5.9 million per year just to conform to the Freedom of Information Act as amended in 1975. For the federal government, as a whole, that adjustment totaled at least $20 million.[23] However, adjustments were more than just monetary for that new agenda item. The Defense Contract Audit Agency found, as a result of the Freedom of Information Act, that both internal administrative decisions and external relationships with the contractors the agency audited were affected. DCAA auditors and audit managers had to make legal decisions about releasing information without legal assistance in the field. And they had to make decisions under penalty of sixty-day suspensions should any refusals be judged arbitrary and capricious. Contractor relationships became strained because of an unwillingness on their part to supply sensitive records that could become public once in DCAA's possession. This led to long delays in gaining information and long negotiations about what material should be subject to audit. The organization was also forced, by the courts, to release its Contract Audit Manual to those who requested it, a move that bureau officials felt was "giving the playbook to the opposition."

The example of DCAA is a typical illustration of the impact of the new agenda on bureaus. As organizations, bureaus will be affected throughout by each of these agenda items advancing to program status. Internal relationships and client relationships will be affected and strained. Everybody will have to readjust at a personal and financial cost. The bureau may no longer be capable of business as usual.

However, readjustment will occur and new relationships will be reestablished. If bureaus cooperate with those promoting new items for their agendas, new routines will certainly develop. After all, the items are what is new because new agendas have emerged before with changes in society and politics. For instance, bureaus of the U.S. Department of Agriculture operated all their programs for research and educational purposes into the 1930's. But, with the emergence of the Depression, they adjusted to deal with a new agenda of price supports, production controls, emergency credit, soil conservation, and rural electrification. Now these items are the "old agenda"; and the fears that present day bureaucrats hold are nothing more than the fears about what will happen along the way as today's new agenda becomes the old agenda of the future.

And their fears are justified. They are justified because the new agenda reflects interest and values that have been largely ignored in the past. The poor, the consumer, minorities, and women have not been accorded equal consideration by government. These fears are justified because the new agenda reflects elements of human awareness that previously have not been a part of public bureaucracy—ecology, worker safety, nutrition, open government. Indeed, rapid evolution is the order of the day in American politics, and the new agenda confronting bureaucrats forces them to speed up and keep in step with many of those changes.

SUMMARY

Although the 1976 presidential campaign had a decidedly anti-bureaucratic flavor to it, the candidates did not reach the voters through such appeals. In fact, the candidates backed off from their earlier zeal for the issue as the campaign wore along.

However, campaign promises to reorganize the federal bureaucracy had been made; and new President Carter appeared convinced that reorganization could bring economy and efficiency to what he considered a wasteful administrative system. So, to save face with the voters and to satisfy his desires for change, Carter ordered a reorganization. That reorganization occurred, through gradual tinkering, but did very little to change the nature of bureaucracy or the way it operated. There were no massive budget, program, or personnel cuts. There were no massive program or bureau shifts. To a great extent, the whole reorganization was cosmetic in purpose and symbolic in style. The major change—the creation of the Department of Energy—was really through addition rather than reorganizing; and it reflected the reliance of government on bureaucracy more than anything else.

Little more could have been expected. Carter could give little personal attention to the reorganization because of the large number of pressing issues confronting him as well as his troubles with Congress. In addition, the mammoth nature of the job demanded internal bureaucratic coordination which, in effect, left the bureaucracy to reorder itself.

A more substantial threat to bureau operations has been going on more quietly than, but at the same time as, the hoopla of electioneering and reorganizing. Bureaucracy is, in fact, changing as it confronts a new agenda. In many issue areas, new agenda items are being brought to bureaus by nonclientele interest groups and other bureaus administering federal regulations. These new items reflect the political changes going on in society as a result of the demands of new political activists and an emerging public awareness about frequently neglected issues. As a result, the content of older public programs has been modified by the need to consider such things as the environment, pollution, occupational safety, health standards, nutrition, the consumer, civil rights, and union activities in government. To some extent, all of these issues now have an impact on the development and implementation of most bureaus' programs. And that is a major political change.

9...

FUTURE PROSPECTS:
A Conclusion about Public Bureaucracy

The mood of the electorate, the complaints of so many presidential candidates, promises of reorganization, and the emergence of "new agenda" items—all of these factors indicate a potential for future governmental reform of bureaucracy. Even if citizen demands are unlikely to pressure reforms, President Carter is in a position to use their sentiments and claim a "national mandate" to act. Under such a threat, the Congress will continue to find it difficult to resist cooperation with reform efforts. If events at the state level are analogous to those at the federal, and they seem to be, such a scenario seems entirely possible. Several states have recently reorganized their bureaucracies through such a strategy; and a number of others are using administrative techniques like management by objectives to bring about reform. Even liberal governors like Edmund Brown, Jr., of California and Michael Dukakis of Massachusetts have attempted to facilitate changes by employing such a strategy.

However, the nature of reforms must be considered. At present, proposals for change deal exclusively with formal structural arrangements and related problems. Reorganization, for example, becomes defined as a plan to consolidate bureaus; and consolidation is intended to reduce overlapping functions, save money, and make it easier to understand which bureau has what specific responsibilities. Reforms in this area are indisputably necessary. An Ohio governor once observed that his state had 23 cabinet level departments, 87 bureaus and agencies, and 212 boards and commissions. "It took us a year and a half to track them all down and see if they existed and were doing anything."[1] Not only governors are confused, so are citizens who must get assistance or rulings in certain problem areas. Their task is often impossible. For example, prior to then

Governor Jimmy Carter's reorganization of Georgia's bureaucracy, there were 22 bureaus dealing with water problems and 7 responsible for special education for deaf children.[2] Citizens who contacted these bureaus often received contradictory rulings and different interpretations of eligibility for assistance. Services were frequently duplicative, and just as often others were overlooked by bureau officials who mistakenly believed some other bureau was in charge. Order, the very purpose of rules and regulations, was missing in the implementation of Georgia programs. Some of the same chaos is found in most other bureaucratic structures as well.

Also hard to fault are the other reforms proposed by President Carter's Reorganization Project. Beyond moving boxes around on organization charts, Carter's plans concentrate on minimizing statistical data, improving the delivery of intergovernmental services, better cash management, and a host of other administrative problems. Yet economy and efficiency are still the primary goals relative to these concerns, just as they are with basic reorganizing.

Despite the general need for some reforms of this kind, it is insufficient to dwell on just the *formal* aspects of bureaucracy in assessing the necessity for change. Bureaus, as they have been presented throughout this book, are important because they provide the information that other political decision-makers need in choosing from among the many possible alternative programs. Decision-makers depend on bureaus for the programs they must produce, and they listen to bureaucrats in order to lower the personal cost of making programmatic choices. This reduces the risk of making the wrong decision. It also gives bureau officials a great amount of *informal* influence and power. But it also poses a series of very important questions for representative democracy. Can formally elected officials ever get bureaus to produce the kinds of programs that they and their constituents prefer? How are citizen preferences translated into government programs, especially if formal control is weak? What determines the bureaucrat's definition of responsible behavior? There are no final answers to any of the above questions that resolve the problem of representation; but reflecting on the implications of all of them is very necessary for all citizens interested in the operation of government. If questions of this sort are neglected, the ultimate impact of bureaucracy could well be a nearly total divorce between public programs and what citizens want. Reorganizing a chaotic bureaucracy, developing new management techniques, saving money, eliminating a few burdensome regulations, and coordinating programs are all necessary. But it is far more important to recognize the basic contradictions between bureaucracy and principles of American democracy and move to control for the disparities. This need was clearly stated by former President Ford when asked to comment about Carter's reorganization one year after his leaving office. "Significant reforms," he maintained, "are rarely undertaken and instead we rely on government reorganization and the appointment of new administrators. Anyone familiar with the Washington bureaucracy knows that just shifting boxes around on an organization chart and putting new bodies in old jobs, without a commitment to a different philosophy and a new statutory framework, will do about as much good in the long term as appointing another study commission."

POLITICAL RESPONSIBILITY

In a democracy, elected representatives should rule. But can they when dependence on bureau information is so high? More and more, it appears that *knowledge is power*, perhaps the greatest power. That is the main lesson taught by this book and alluded to by Mr. Ford.

The growth of bureaucratic government affects representative institutions, as earlier chapters have made clear, in five important ways.

1. The person who occupies the White House is not the "civics book president" exerting personal influence on a vast array of public programs. Any president's influence is limited to a few key programs, and even there his success will be greatly dependent on the abilities of his closest advisors. The same applies to governors and mayors. Chief executives accept most programs on face value and approve them just as they were developed and submitted by bureaus.

2. Chief executives are almost entirely unable to direct detailed and comprehensive policies. The fragmented control that bureaus have over programs nearly precludes coordination; and bureau resources and allies prevent their being forced to comply.

3. Most issues before legislatures are neglected by all but a handful of members. Specialization paralleling that of the bureaucracy is a major legislative feature, and legislators tend to listen and follow the advice of those colleagues who gain expertise. Without bureaus, however, legislators would seldom be able to acquire the information and data they need to become opinion leaders.

4. Intergovernmental control over programs leaves no single level of government in charge, since these programs are designed to be cooperative ventures. This divided authority has the corresponding effect of further eroding the controls of executives and legislators who must share power with those at other levels. However, the real ability to negotiate intergovernmental programs usually rests in the hands of bureau officials who administer the programs on a daily basis. These are the individuals who approve projects and arrange compromises when disagreements arise.

5. For all practical purposes, the courts are powerless in changing the substantive decisions about bureau programs. They provide no final resort to citizens who feel unfairly treated by the allocation of public goods and services.

The American political system, as characterized by these factors, is not one that citizens easily hold in check. Neither the "separation of powers" nor "federalism" truly provides citizens with alternate institutions for obtaining their preferences. Citizens may have different institutions to go to, but all of them are in effect interrelated through bureau ties. Presidents, governors, and legislators all rely on what bureau findings term feasible. The planning role of the bureau has effectively penetrated each institution and each level of government.

That situation would present no problem for representative government if elected officials thought of themselves as "delegates."[3] However, officeholders have long rejected the confining role of the "delegate" who rejects and accepts programs on the basis of what the electorate wants. Elected officials feel their own informed instincts are better guides than public opinion. Or they feel other political participants can tell them more about a program's impact than citizens back home. After all, there is no way to systematically judge what voters want between elections; and many citizens are perceived as uninformed anyway.

As a result, elected officials look for credible assistance from colleagues, staff members, lobbyists, and bureaucrats who are willing and able to provide it. Of all these sources, the bureau is the most legitimate and usually the best informed. And it can provide information indirectly through each of the other sources when direct access is precluded. That, in fact, is what normally happens when a legislator relies on a respected colleague or when a governor takes the word of his staff.

Elected officials can hardly be called responsive to citizen pressures when they must often follow the lead of bureaucrats. Bureaus are not under control. Instead they share control with executives, legislators, and citizens. Bureaus have institutionalized a place for themselves in American politics, and they have secured resources to protect their place. No matter who becomes president or who is elected to a congressional seat, there will be little impact on the programs of most bureaus. The bureaucracy is too extensively involved and two deeply in control for great changes to come about. Stated another way, elections will not transform bureaucracy. At most, electoral politics will only put new individuals in power to bargain with those who remain.

PUBLIC SERVICE

Bureaucrats are typically referred to as public servants. They do, of course, provide public services. But do bureau officials provide them at public request under public directives? That answer is "yes" and "no," depending on how the public is defined.

Earlier chapters have shown that bureaucratic government responds to directives from the citizenry in three ways.

1. Political party differences do exist on some programs. Bureaucrats follow party preferences when they identify with the party personally or when an elected official makes an issue of a party position. However, bureaucrats tend to avoid partisan positions in their planning. And there is certainly no mechanism for translating party platform positions into bureau directives after electoral victors are declared.[4] Winners can negotiate with bureaus any way they please.

2. Interest groups exchange information and political support with bureaus when a compromise can be arranged. In fact, compromises by both groups and bureaus are encouraged in order to avoid costly political conflict. However, compromises generally are restricted to interest groups and bureaus who share a common concern and who have collected information to bolster their respective positions. Groups outside the appropriate "whirlpool" have an extremely difficult time challenging a bureau's information, expertise, and political legitimacy.

3. Groups of citizens and even individuals can obtain desired results from bureaus by making it easier for bureau officials to serve them than to ignore them. Such citizens can pressure elected officials to contact a bureau on their behalf, tie the office up with "red tape," or just bother bureaucrats so much that they give in to their demands in order to get rid of the complainants.[5]

Bureaus, in other words, respond to political resources just as they force elected officials to respond to those of the bureau. That does not mean that a bureau's officials ignore the purpose for which the bureau was intended. Nor does it mean that bureaucrats neglect those who attempt to use the bureau's service but who cannot pressure its officials into compliance. Of course not.

The need for resources to affect the bureau does mean that some segments of the public will get exceptional services. These citizens will be able to get officials within the bureau to listen to them while developing and modifying programs. And the changes will be to their advantage. The same people will promptly receive services even if bureau rules need be slanted in their favor to do so. Other clients will have to wait, take their turn, and follow the present rules. These resourceless citizens are at the mercy of a bureau's routine procedures.[6]

The fact of political life is that a program's benefits are not distributed equally to the public as a whole. Bureaus operate according to set procedures. They gather data, make recommendations, implement their programs, and change things according to resulting routines. Citizens who can break down the routines and exercise leadership get the most while the rest of a bureau's clients must follow the rules. In other words, a select portion of the public directs programs to the extent that they can force compromises.

Routines are determined by bureau officials for their own operating ease. Procedures are seldom revised because of directives from elected representatives, officials, or supervisory bureaucrats. When complaints from such sources are presented, it usually leads to a circumvention of the routines rather than reform. As a result, unequal treatment continues to be extended to clients who can back their demands the hardest.

THE PARTICIPANT'S DILEMMA

Bureau officials as they have been portrayed through this text are not inherently evil men. They neither intend to discriminate against segments of the population nor do they aspire to avoid the programs citizens want. But, as we have continuously seen, several organizational imperatives often lead them to precisely those results.

As organizations, bureaus have several needs which affect the behavior of their personnel.[7]

1. A bureau's programs are its life's blood. Without programs, a bureau has no need for personnel; and if programs are lost, jobs normally go as well. For that reason, bureau officials are inclined to be positive about what they do. They look for strong points about present programs, they emphasize contributions rather than failures, and they are inclined to accept rather weak indicators as evidence of program successes. When identifying new programs to replace old ones, bureau officials tend to be concerned about minimizing the loss of jobs and maximizing the bureau's opportunity for gaining extra ones. If clients or other citizens are negative about a bureau's aspirations or performance, its officials can only feel threatened. As a result, bureaucrats will attempt to improve their performance to avoid conflict. Or they will present evidence to refute the charges, contend that citizen opponents know very little about the bureau's problems, and generally argue that experts know best.

2. Any bureau has limited supplies of man-hours, personal energy, and

money to allocate to its programs. However, these resources are all some-what elastic. Employees can work overtime without pay, and they can fight for supplemental appropriations if the bureau's supplies are ex-hausted. Both of these demanding activities increase the costs of the job by making it more difficult, however. Under other conditions, employees can take it somewhat easy in their work if their bureau has more than enough personnel, and they can sometimes save money which can be allocated elsewhere for more desirable purchases. These features make the job more pleasant.

Bureau officials will prefer to have some excess in available supplies; and they will most certainly oppose overextension. As a result, pressures from clients are treated differently according to the availability of time, energy, and money. If clients want program reform, it will likely be forth-coming when some slack, or excess, exists. But the more bureau officials are pressed to reach or exceed their limits, the more resistance clients get. When such a condition exists, the bureau is unlikely to develop new pro-grams or revise the implementation of old ones. Instead, clients will stand in line; and bureau officials will defend the lines by pointing to a lack of executive or legislative support which would allow increased expenditures.

3. Political allies are the ones who keep a bureau's programs operating. Executives, legislators, staff personnel, and lobbyists can all be crucial when it comes time for extending a program or refunding it. Therefore, to protect its programs, a bureau worries more about what its allies and supporters want from the program than its clients. If the recipients of a program are opposed to the wishes of an important subcommittee chair-man about program operation, for instance, "clients come last."[8]

In a sense, the bureaucrat's role as "organization man" confronts his role as "public servant." Bureaucrats have more to do than operate pro-grams. They must maintain their bureau as well. Even in conserving re-sources, bureau officials are looking for more than personal ease. They are concerned with organizational needs as well. Bureaus that make undue demands on their employees take a chance on losing the best of them when more appealing jobs appear elsewhere. In addition, budget overruns threaten the bureau's political security by suggesting that its officials cannot manage annual appropriations. No bureau can make a practice of such requests, because congressional watchdogs will soon intervene.

These two roles, "organization man" and "public servant," are not all that indistinct, however. If a bureau official ignores organizational necessities in favor of serving clients, he really threatens nothing more than the bureau's long-term ability to provide goods and services. Bureaus cannot provide the present level of benefits if personnel and funds are stripped away. So, to serve the public is to serve the organization; but to serve the organization is to place the public's concern last. That is the paradoxical dilemma confronting all bureau officials. None can escape it as long as there is a need to protect the political resources that give the bureau strength, and that is precisely the goal of the bureau when it works to maintain its "whirlpool" alliances.

AND FINALLY, THE FUTURE WILL BE THE PRESENT

In the future, political decisions in America probably will be made very much as they are now. That is to say, the near divorce between the ballot box and the allocation of societal benefits will neither be finalized nor reconciled. Citizens will not be voting for officials who can massively redirect public programs, yet programs will be influenced by the preferences of elected representatives. Yet influence will never be solely in the hands of elected officials. Chief executives and legislators have no alternative but to continue their dependency on bureaus and will always share power as a result.

The present situation seems likely to continue despite the proposal of several reforms that will go far beyond reorganizing bureaucratic structures. In fact, a small number of general reforms for bureau control undoubtedly will be adopted; but their effect will be marginal because the generic problems of reconciling bureaucracy and democracy are inescapable. Although predicting specific changes is impossible, several prominent ones call for improving legislator information sources, minimizing bureaucratic regulations, and reallocating power to citizen groups. Three specific proposals that have attracted some advocates are outlined below in order to show that reforms designed to correct one imbalance are impractical because they tip the scale elsewhere.

1. *One way to decrease the dependence of legislators is to increase the size of their staffs.* Only a multiple growth in staff could ever match the planning and research capabilities of present bureaus, and it seems unlikely that government would support such growth. It would be too expensive and too great a duplication of the administrative bureaucracy.

At best, staff increases will only allow legislators to have their own experienced employees work more closely with bureau officials. Such cooperation obviously could be of help in supervising bureaus. However, that help would probably be very limited. To a great extent, large staff increases would further lead to a legislative bureaucracy. Committee and personal staff members increasingly would specialize, they would look to make careers of their work, and they would develop very close ties with regular bureau and interest group contacts.[9] In short, a legislative bureaucracy would mean that staff loyalty to a particular legislator would be weak and of secondary concern. These bureaucrats would also be worried about the ease of their job and the continuity of their positions once their legislative employers are replaced in office.

2. *The best way to decrease bureau control over programs is to eliminate the discretion bureau officials have in developing and implementing them.* Revenue sharing and a negative income tax both could conceivably have that effect. Instead of developing a housing program through the Department of Housing and Urban Development, the federal government could just send out money for local governments to build their own. Rather than operating poverty programs, the federal government could mail checks to the poor and guarantee them a certain income level.

However, revenue sharing only shifts the construction burden to local bureaucracies that would have to grow immensely to replace the skills of federal employees. And a negative income tax would not ensure adequate housing, food, or education for its recipients. While those results are not necessarily condemnations of the plans, they do appear to be problems for both appointed and elected politicians. Federal officials, presidents, congressmen, and bureaucrats would all give up most of their control if federal programs just sent money. That would be an undesirable result for all federal participants, and unless some of these officials decide that it is better to live without influence and responsibility, future plans of this sort probably will have regulatory "strings attached." For example, rules may require cities to construct certain types of housing and meet federal building standards. And others will limit what the poor can purchase and own. They may also be told what living standards must be met for funding to continue. Of course if regulations of that sort are imposed, bureaucrats as well as other officials will have plenty to do and a good bit of influence and discretion over programmatic content and the lives of clients.

3. *Involving citizens in program development and project design could get bureaucrats to listen to clients' ideas.* Over the past several years, citizen participation of this sort has been encouraged by the federal government. Citizens from the local community are selected for advisory boards and consulted at each stage in the program by officials in charge. This plan means, in effect, that bureau officials do their work with citizen assistance.

Several problems exist with the plan, however. In the first place, citizen boards usually lack any formal powers. But, even if they did have a veto over bureau recommendations, citizens are put in a difficult situation when they must work with bureau experts. As advisors, citizens usually lack research skills and information about the program's content and purpose. As a result, citizen boards are oftentimes easily led and even intimidated.

Other participatory problems exist from the bureau's perspective. Some citizens might only want to stop a bureau's programs. Or they might be trying to use their board positions as stepping stones for personal influence in the community. For these reasons, bureaus normally play some role in the selection of board members.

No matter what happens, however, citizen participation presents a representational dilemma. Citizens might represent the community better than bureaucrats, but they might not. If bureaus select members or if citizens use the boards for their political purposes, there is still no guarantee that those who need a program's benefits are being given a chance to affect their allocation. Because of these many problems, citizen participation of this kind will probably always have a minimal influence on the content and implementation of public programs. It seems difficult to believe that these boards will ever provide institutionalized power to citizens in the decision-making process.

Reform proposals like the three above would not only fail to link bureaus more closely to the electorate; they would also be disruptive to most decision-makers. Therefore, the likelihood that radically redistributive reforms will pass is quite remote. It should be remembered that bureaus are important because they contribute information and assistance to those who pass legislation. Since all decision-makers depend on bureaus for something, no one is advantaged by limiting disruption or otherwise interfering with their contributions. That is, it is to no one's advantage except citizens who desire more of a voice in determining the content and impact of public programs.

Major changes will only occur when all the components of the governmental system change their orientation toward bureaucracy. Conceivably, two factors could bring this about. One, citizens could become aroused and make bureau control a key campaign issue forcing politicians to change the rules. Or, two, financial resources would become so scarce that government could no longer afford to maintain a substantial number of ongoing public programs. In that instance, controls would be indirectly the result of societal pressures as elected politicians reviewed bureaucratic offerings in order to trim and cut those programs that would generate the least political pressure.

Such conditions are not too likely to come about. The latter would demand an economic collapse of great proportions, greater than even previous depressions. Presently, too many financial reductions can be made without serious loss of entire programs. Decades of unfettered budgetary growth has brought most bureaus to the point where, even if excesses are not common, they have the latitude to shift budgetary priorities and still keep most programs intact. In a selective fashion, bureaus can cut back on projects, close the least productive or desirable facilities, freeze hiring, increase staff reductions, and incrementally cut overhead operations. Even a funding reduction of several percentage points would not necessarily limit the delivery of public goods and services to the extent that most clients would notice. The second change requires an even more sweeping change, a recognition by the citizenry that bureaucrats really matter. This would necessitate an extensive reeducation of a public that thinks of bureaucrats as powerless and believes in either conspiracy theories or the absolute authority of one man at the top.

SUMMARY

In the final analysis, it appears that only a continued reorganization like that noted in Chapter 8 is likely, and not a change in the way Americans depend on bureaucracy. This does not mean that bureaus will never be better able to satisfy society. On the contrary, tomorrow's bureaucracy could potentially perform better even without externally imposed reform. In the future, it appears that bureaucrats will be able to develop more realistic indicators for determining program needs. In addition, non-quantitative, but nonetheless systematic, analysis will be refined to overcome the disadvantages of soft programs.[10] On the whole, knowledge about the way things are and the way programs work will improve. Bureaus can never be eliminated, nor is it likely that they will be saddled with controls that bog their operation down. In the future, bureaucrats will know and understand more, do a better job because of it, and keep citizens relatively happy. And this will occur because bureau officials, as they always have, will recognize that better performance allows them more freedom from political pressure and thus more latitude in doing things their way. After all, bureaus gained political influence in this manner, and they can best keep it by continuing to capitalize on their strengths and advantages.

Certainly reliance on the capabilities and goodwill of bureau experts is no guarantee that citizens will be able to get what they want from government. Nor is it really a guarantee that they will get everything they really need. But no amount of bureaucratic reform will produce such guarantees either, especially if the changes leave intact, as they must, a bureaucracy that is capable of doing the work society and the rest of government expects and must have. It is finally necessary to conclude that an effective bureaucracy is in large part uncontrollable except by a society that is extremely knowledgeable about its programmatic needs and about what both government in general and bureaucracy in particular are doing to meet them. As noted in Chapter 8, new agenda items and new approaches to public problems emerged through the forceful demands of advocates of specialized change. Even when government listens and responds, some abuses will go on, because perfect knowledge by any citizen or group is impossible and some officials will try to take advantage of that fact. In the end the best advice is probably the simplest— citizens must be vigilant, they must seek out information, and, above all else, they should continue to be suspicious of bureaucrats and their goals.

NOTES

1. BUREAUCRACY, BUREAUS, AND PROGRAMS

1. Dwight Waldo, "Organization Theory: An Elephantine Problem," *Public Administration Review* (December, 1961), p. 220.

2. Max Weber, "The Essentials of Bureaucratic Behavior: An Ideal-Type Construct," in Robert Merton et al. (eds.), *Reader in Bureaucracy* (New York: Free Press, 1952).

3. David Schuman, *Bureaucracies, Organizations, and Administration* (New York: Macmillan Publishing Co., 1976), p. 56.

4. Ibid.

5. Frederick W. Taylor, *The Principles of Scientific Management* (New York: Harper and Row, 1947).

6. Paul Appleby, *Policy and Administration* (University, Alabama: University of Alabama Press, 1949), p. 7.

7. David Easton, *The Political System* (New York: Alfred A. Knopf, 1953), p. 129. Easton says that this is "the essential property of that complex of activity, called political, that over the years men have sought to understand."

8. Office of the Federal Register, National Archives and Records Service, General Services Administration, *United States Government Manual* (Washington, D.C., Government Printing Office, July 1977).

9. Op. cit.

10. Anthony Downs, *Inside Bureaucracy* (Boston: Little, Brown, 1967), p. 1.

11. Federal Council for Science and Technology, Committee on Domestic Technology Transfer, *Directory of Federal Technology Transfer* (Washington, D.C., Government Printing Office, June 1975), p. 57.

12. Op. cit.

13. James W. Davis, *An Introduction to Public Administration* (New York: Free Press, 1974), p. 11.

14. This can best be seen in the excellent book by Alice Rivlin, *Systematic Thinking for Social Action* (Washington, D.C.: Brookings Institution, 1971).

15. Malcolm E. Jewell and Samuel C. Patterson, *The Legislative Process in the United States* (New York: Random House, 1966), pp. 330-331.

16. David Truman, *The Governmental Process* (New York: Alfred A. Knopf, 1951).

17. *New York*, November 25, 1974.

18. John Wahlke, Heinz Eulau, William Buchanan, and Leroy Ferguson, *The Legislative System* (New York: John Wiley and Sons, 1962), pp. 141-169.

19. J. Leiper Freeman, *The Political Process: Executive Bureau-Legislative Committee Relations* (New York: Random House, 1955); Charles M. Hardin, "Agricultural Price Policy: The Political Role of Bureaucracy," in Don F. Hadwiger and William P. Browne (eds.), *The New Politics of Food* (Lexington, Massachusetts: D. C. Heath and Company, 1978).

20. U.S. Civil Service Commission, "The Federal Career Service," pamphlet (1969).

21. Downs, loc. cit.

22. Ibid.

23. Herbert Simon, *Administrative Behavior* (New York: Free Press, 1945), pp. 12-13.

2. THE BUREAU OF MINES AT WORK

1. *United States Government Manual, 1974-1975* (Washington, D.C.: U.S. Government Printing Office), p. 271.

2. Federal Council for Science and Technology, Committee on Domestic Technology Transfer, *Directory of Federal Technology Transfer* (Washington, D.C.: U.S. Government Printing Office, 1975), pp. 123-127.

3. *U.S. Government Manual, 1974-1975*, p. 281.

4. BOM is quite sensitive to charges of negligence in the area of safety and constantly alludes in bureau publications to its long-time commitment to health and safety goals. It is, however, impossible to substantiate bureau claims beyond identifying a few token research efforts. The mining industry certainly felt little pressure from BOM on safety matters; nor did it work with the bureau to develop and refine safety techniques prior to the late 1960's.

5. *U.S. Government Manual, 1974-1975*, , p. 287.

6. An excellent recounting of Bureau-industrial relations is in a book by Robert Engler, *The Politics of Oil* (Chicago: University of Chicago Press, 1961).

7. Ibid., p. 104.

8. Michael Barone, Grant Ujifusa, Douglas Matthews, *The Almanac of American Politics, 1976* (New York: E. P. Dutton, 1975), pp. 955, 971.

3. POLITICAL INSTITUTIONS AND THE BUREAU

1. David Halberstam, *The Best and the Brightest* (New York: Random House, 1969).

2. Graham T. Allison, *Essence of Decision* (Boston: Little, Brown, 1971), pp. 141-142.

3. Ibid., pp. 123-124.

4. Theodore H. White, *The Making of the President 1968* (New York: Atheneum, 1969), p. 183.

5. For the most recent account see James W. Davis and Delbert Ringquist, *President and Congress: Toward a New Power Balance* (New York: Barron's, 1975).

6. Nick Kotz, *Let Them Eat Promises* (Englewood Cliffs, New Jersey: Prentice-Hall, 1969), p. 80.

7. See Richard F. Fenno, Jr., *Congressmen in Committees* (Boston: Little, Brown, 1973).

8. Kotz, op. cit., p. 83.

9. Ibid., p. 89.

10. Lester Milbrath, *The Washington Lobbyists* (New York: Rand McNally, 1963).

11. Unpublished quote from research study of urban interest groups by the author, 1971.

12. Herbert Simon, Donald L. Smithburg, and Victor Thompson, *Public Administration* (New York: Alfred A. Knopf, 1950), p. 461.
13. Douglass Cater, *Power in Washington* (New York: Random House, 1964).
14. Ernest Griffith, *The Impasse of Democracy* (New York: Harrison-Hilton, 1939).
15. This material is derived from unpublished research on the Law Enforcement Assistance Administration. William P. Browne, "Regionalization and Bureaucracy: The Law Enforcement Assistance Administration in Transition" (1974); Thomas E. Cronin, "Presidents, the Crime Issue and the War on Crime" (1973).
16. President's Commission on Law Enforcement and Administration of Justice, *The Challenge of Crime in a Free Society* (Washington, D.C.: U.S. Government Printing Office, 1967).
17. Nicholas Katzenbach, Hearings on Presidential Commissions, U.S. Senate, May 26, 1971, Subcommittee on Administrative Practice and Procedure, Committee on the Judiciary, p. 122.

4. BUREAUS AND THE BUREAUCRACY

1. Murray Weidenbaum, *The Modern Public Sector* (New York: Basic Books, 1969), p. 15.
2. Allen Schick, "A Death in the Bureaucracy: The Demise of PPB," *Public Administration Review* (March-April 1973), pp. 146-156; Allen Schick, *Budget Innovation in the States* (Washington, D.C.: Brookings Institution, 1971).
3. Gordon Tullock, *The Politics of Bureaucracy* (Washington, D.C.: General Affairs Press, 1965); pp. 137-141.
4. Richard Fenno, *The President's Cabinet* (Cambridge, Massachusetts: Harvard University Press, 1959).
5. Peter Blau and W. Richard Scott, *Formal Organizations* (San Francisco: Chandler Publishing, 1962), pp. 116-139.
6. Anthony Downs, *Inside Bureaucracy* (Boston: Little, Brown, 1966), pp. 211-215.
7. National League of Cities and the U.S. Conference of Mayors, *The Mayor and Manpower* (Washington, D.C.: 1970).
8. Morton Grodzins, *The American System: A New View of Government in the United States* (Chicago: Rand McNally, 1966).
9. This material is derived from unpublished research on the Law Enforcement Assistance Administration. William P. Browne, "Regionalization and Bureaucracy: The Law Enforcement Assistance Administration in Transition" (1974); Thomas E. Cronin, "Presidents, the Crime Issue and the War on Crime" (1973).

5. DEVELOPING PROGRAMS IN A MAZE

1. This point is well made by David R. Mayhew, *Congress: The Electoral Connection* (New Haven, Connecticut: Yale University Press, 1974).
2. Unpublished quote from author's research on LEAA, 1974.
3. James W. Davis and Randall B. Ripley, "The Bureau of the Budget and Executive Branch Agencies: Notes on their Interaction," *Journal of Politics* (November, 1967), pp. 749-769.
4. *LEAA: Fifth Annual Report of the Law Enforcement Assistance Administration* (Washington, D.C.: U.S. Government Printing Office, 1973), p. 97.
5. Ibid., pp. 3-4.
6. Nick Kotz, *Let Them Eat Promises* (Englewood Cliffs, New Jersey: Prentice-Hall, 1969), pp. 186-187.
7. Ida R. Hoos, *Systems Analysis for Public Policy* (Berkeley: University of California Press, 1972).

8.   Alice Rivlin, *Systematic Thinking for Social Action* (Washington, D.C.: Brookings Institution, 1971), pp. 9-16.
9.   Ibid., pp. 91-119.
10.   Planning aides are constantly taking note of this perceptual problem. See for example National League of Cities and United States Conference of Mayors, *Planning and Management Guide for City Officials* (Washington, D.C.: 1974).
11.   Raymond Bauer (ed.), *Social Indicators* (Cambridge, Massachusetts: MIT Press, 1966).
12.   Anthony Downs, *Inside Bureaucracy* (Boston: Little, Brown, 1966).
13.   Richard Fenno, *The Power of the Purse: Appropriation Politics in Congress* (Boston: Little, Brown, 1966), pp. 264-314.

6. OPERATING GOVERNMENT PROGRAMS

1.   Jeffrey Pressman and Aaron Wildavsky, *Implementation: How Great Expectations in Washington are Dashed in Oakland* (Berkeley: University of California Press, 1973). This is a singular exception to that statement.
2.   Almost all of the pre-1960's literature on public administration conforms to that dichotomy. See for instance Dwight Waldo, *The Administrative State* (New York: Ronald Press, 1948).
3.   *United States Government Manual* (Washington, D.C.: U.S. Government Printing Office, 1974), p. 379.
4.   Harold Watts, "Adjusted and Extended Preliminary Results from the Urban Graduated Work Incentive Experiment" (Madison: University of Wisconsin, Institute for Research on Poverty, 1970), p. 40; Joseph Pechman and Michael Timpane (eds.), *Work Incentives and Income Guarantee: The New Jersey Negative Income Experiment* (Washington, D.C.: Brookings Institution, 1975).
5.   Alice Rivlin, *Systematic Thinking for Social Action* (Washington, D.C.: Brookings Institution, 1971), pp. 96-100.
6.   F. J. Roethlisberger and W. J. Dickson, *Management and the Worker* (Cambridge, Massachusetts: Harvard University Press, 1939).
7.   Martin Meyerson and Edward Banfield, *Politics, Planning, and the Public Interest* ((New York: Free Press, 1955); Harold Wolman, *The Politics of Federal Housing* (New York: Dodd, Mead, 1970.
8.   David Murray, "Ted: Viet Evacuation 'Ill-conceived, Poorly Implemented,'" *Chicago Sun-Times* (May 14, 1975), p. 26.
9.   Ibid.
10.   Charles Lindblom, "The Science of 'Muddling Through,'" *Public Administration Review* (Spring, 1959), pp. 79-88; Otto Davis, M. A. H. Dempster and Aaron Wildavsky, "A Theory of the Budgetary Process," *American Political Science Review* (September, 1966) pp. 529-574.
11.   Harold Wilensky, *Organizational Intelligence* (New York: Basic Books, 1967), pp. 8-40.
12.   Murray, op. cit.
13.   Richard Fenno, *The Power of the Purse: Appropriation Politics in Congress* (Boston: Little, Brown, 1966), pp. 291-293.
14.   This information on the evacuation of Saigon is from the author's interviews with marines involved in the program.
15.   Jeanne Lowe, *Cities in a Race with Time* (New York: Random House, 1967). pp. 110-163.
16.   Pressman and Wildavsky, op. cit.
17.   Meyerson and Banfield, op. cit.
18.   See for example, Frances Fox Piven and Richard Cloward, *Regulating the Poor* (New York: Pantheon Books, 1971).
19.   John R. Gist, "Mandatory Expenditures and the Defense Sector: Theory of

Budgetary Incrementalism," *Sage Professional Papers in American Politics*, vol. 2, 04-020 (Beverly Hills, California: Sage Publications, 1974), pp. 8-9.

20.   The development of planning, programming and budgeting systems as well as use of management by objectives are both indicators of this trend. As financial resources become more scarce, accountability can be expected to increase.

21.   James W. Davis, *An Introduction to Public Administration* (New York: Free Press, 1974), p. 288.

22.   Raymond A. Bauer (ed.), *Social Indicators* (Cambridge: MIT Press, 1966), pp. 1-67.

23.   Evaluation is almost as ignored as implementation by students of public bureaucracies and government programs. Exceptions to this rule include the excellent chapter by James W. Davis, op. cit., pp. 271-288; Carol Weiss, *Evaluation Research* (Englewood Cliffs, N.J.: Prentice Hall, 1972); and Carol Weiss (ed.), *Evaluating Action Programs* (Boston: Allyn and Bacon, 1972).

7. BUREAUCRACY'S IRON GLOVE: REGULATION

1.   Glen O. Robinson and Ernest Gellhorn, *The Administrative Process* (St. Paul, Minnesota: West Publishing, 1974), pp. 103-104.

2.   Philippe Nonet, *Administrative Justice* (New York: Russell Sage Foundation, 1969), p. 3.

3.   Roscoe Pound, *Administrative Law* (Pittsburgh: University of Pittsburgh Press, 1942).

4.   Ernest Gellhorn, *Administrative Law and Process in a Nutshell* (St. Paul, Minnesota: West Publishing, 1972), pp. 127-128. Citing Section 4, 5 U.S.C.A. Section 553 (b), (c), (d).

5.   Ibid., p. 127.

6.   Ibid., p. 132.

7.   Robert E. Cushman, *The Independent Regulatory Commissions* (Fairlawn, New Jersey: Oxford University Press, 1941), chapter 3.

8.   Robinson, op. cit., p. 33.

9.   Gellhorn, op. cit., p. 49.

10.   Robinson, op. cit., p. 33.

11.   *United States Government Manual*, 1974-1975 (Washington, D.C.: U.S. Government Printing Office, 1974).

12.   Nicholas Henry, *Public Administration and Public Affairs* (Englewood Cliffs, New Jersey: Prentice-Hall, 1975), p. 9.

13.   Committee on Administrative Management, *Personnel Administration in the Public Service* (Washington, D.C.: U.S. Government Printing Office, 1937).

8. BUREAUCRACY THREATENED—THE POLITICS OF THE 1970's

1.   Jules Witcover, *Marathon: The Pursuit of the Presidency, 1972-1976* (New York: Viking Press, 1977).

2.   George Gallup, "Federal Workers Held in Low Public Esteem," *Washington Post*, June 12, 1977.

3.   Henry A. Plotkin, "Issues in the 1976 Presidential Campaign" in Gerald Pomper et al., *The Election of 1976* (New York: David McKay Company, 1977), pp. 36-43.

4.   Ibid., pp. 43-47.

5.   *NEA Reporter* (September, 1977), p. 1.

6.   Gerald Pomper, "The Presidential Election" in Gerald Pomper et al., *The Election of 1976* (New York: David McKay Company, 1977), pp. 73-74.

7. Ibid., p. 75.
8. Theodore H. White, *The Making of the President, 1968* (New York: Pocket Books, 1970), pp. 432-436.
9. While not addressing this particular issue, Pomper suggests that the media "overanalyzed and often exaggerated" Carter statements. Pomper, op. cit., p. 67.
10. Ronald C. Moe, *Executive Reorganization: Issue Brief Number IB75014* (Washington, D.C.: Library of Congress, Congressional Research Service, 1977), pp. 3-4.
11. Ibid., p. 18.
12. Michael P. Balzano, *Reorganizing the Federal Bureaucracy: The Rhetoric and the Reality* (Washington, D.C.: American Enterprise Institute, 1977), Chapter 2.
13. Ibid., pp. 33-35.
14. Jean Conley and Joel Havemann, "Reorganization—Two Plans, One Department Down, Much More to Come." *National Journal* (December 3, 1977), p. 1876.
15. Joseph A. Califano, Jr., *A Presidential Nation* (New York: Norton and Sons, 1975), p. 25.
16. Ibid., p. 27.
17. Charles W. Anderson, *Statecraft: An Introduction to Political Choice and Judgement* (New York: John Wiley, 1977), pp. 220-222.
18. Don Paarlberg, "The Farm Policy Agenda" in *Increasing Understanding of Public Problems and Policies—1975* (Chicago: Farm Foundation, 1975), pp. 95-102.
19. Don Paarlberg, "A New Agenda for Agriculture" presented at the 1977 Agricultural Policy Symposium, Washington, D.C.
20. Jeffrey M. Berry, *Lobbying for the People* (Princeton: Princeton University Press, 1977).
21. Roger W. Cobb and Charles D. Elder, *Participation in American Politics: The Dynamics of Agenda-Building* (Boston: Allyn and Bacon, 1972), pp. 110-129.
22. Paarlberg, "The Farm Policy Agenda," Ibid., p. 96.
23. George Lardner, Jr., "Freedom of Information Act: Burdensome, Costly, Much Used." *The Washington Post* (July 25, 1976).

9. FUTURE PROSPECTS: A CONCLUSION ABOUT PUBLIC BUREAUCRACY

1. Neil Peirce, "Structural Reform of Bureaucracy Grows Rapidly," *National Journal* (April 5, 1975), p. 506.
2. Ibid., p. 505.
3. John Wahlke, Heinz Eulau, William Buchanan, and Leroy Ferguson, *The Legislative System* (New York: Wiley, 1962), pp. 272-276.
4. This more than any other factor seems to doom the "responsible party model."
5. Michael Lipsky, *Protest in City Politics* (Chicago: Rand McNally, 1970).
6. Ira Sharkansky, *The Routines of Politics* (New York: Van Nostrand, 1970).
7. This organization is derived from Anthony Downs, *Inside Bureaucracy* (Boston: Little, Brown, 1967).
8. Esther Stanton, *Clients Come Last* (Beverly Hills, California: Sage Publications, 1970). See also Eugene Lewis, *American Politics in a Bureaucratic Age: Citizens, Constituents, Clients and Victims* (Cambridge, Massachusetts: Winthrop Publishing, 1977).
9. This point can be seen in two articles. Thomas Redburn, "Wedding Presents, Cigars, and Deference"; Peter Gruenstein and Daniel West, "Anything You Can Eat, Drink, or Fornicate in One Afternoon," *Washington Monthly* (June, 1975), pp. 4-14.
10. E. S. Quade, *Analysis of Public Decisions* (New York: Elsevier, 1975).

INDEX

Administration and politics, 9-11
Administrative Office of the United
  States Courts, 11
Administrative thought, 7-11
Agricultural Research Service, 91
Agriculture Marketing Service, 15
Agriculture, United States Department
  of, 15, 50, 53, 76, 151, 152, 154,
  155, 157
Air Force, Department of, 47, 54, 76,
  104
Allison, Graham T., 172
American Bar Association, 136
American Farm Bureau Federation, 25
American Mining Congress, 39
Americans for Democratic Action, 58
Anderson, Charles W., 176
Appleby, Paul, 9-10, 171
Army Corps of Engineers, 114
Army, Department of, 94
Ash Council, 136, 137

Balzano, Michael P., 176
Banfield, Edward, 174
Barone, Michael, 172
Bauer, Richard, 174, 175
Bay Area Rapid Transit District, 114
Bayh, Birch, 134
Bergland, Bob, 151-152
Berry, Jeffrey M., 176
Blau, Peter, 173
Boycotts, 155
Brown Jr., Edmund (Jerry), 159
Browne, William P., 172, 173

Brownlow Committee, 135
Brownlow, Louis, 135
Buchanan, William, 172, 176
Budgeting, 12, 19, 50-53, 68-69, 73,
  74, 79, 92-93, 101, 165, 169
Bureau, defined, 11
Bureau resources, defined, 20
Bureaucratic political influence,
  defined, 19-23

Cabinet heads, 61-63, 71-72, 82, 134,
  146, 151, 153
Cahill, William, 62
Califano, Joseph A., 151, 153, 176
Carter, Jimmy, 48-49, 138, 143-144,
  145, 146-153, 158, 159, 160, 161,
  176
Cater, Douglass, 60, 173
Central Intelligence Agency, 90, 145
Citizen participation, 9, 18, 124,
  125-126, 167-168, 170
Civil Service Commission, 172
Civil Service protection, 73
Clark, Ramsey, 61, 62, 82
Cloward, Richard, 174
Cobb, Roger W., 176
Commerce, Department of, 56, 155
Community Planning and Development,
  Bureau of, 124
Congressional Budget Office, 69
Congressional committees, 50-54, 59,
  62, 89, 149
Congressional subcommittees, 39,
  52-53, 62, 108

Conley, Jean, 176
Consumer Federation of America, 155
Consumer Protection Agency, 57
Cronin, Thomas E., 173
Cuba, 46-47
Cushman, Robert E., 175

Davis, James W., 172
Davis, James Warren, 116, 117, 172, 173, 175
Davis, Otto, 174
Defense Contract Audit Agency, 156, 157
Defense, Department of, 17, 47, 145, 156
Dempster, M. A. H., 174
Dickson, W. J., 174
Downs, Anthony, 171, 173, 174, 176
Drug Abuse Policy, Office of, 149, 152
Dukakis, Michael, 159

Easton, David, 171
Economic Advisors, Council for, 66
Economic Development Administration, 11, 113
Economic Opportunity, Office of, 47
Education, Department of, 145, 152
Education, Office of, 13, 16
Educational and Cultural Affairs, Bureau of, 152
Eisenhower, Dwight D., 76, 113, 136
Elder, Charles D., 176
Elementary and Secondary Education, Bureau of, 16
Enabling acts, defined, 18
Energy and Minerals, Office of, 27, 28, 35, 70
Energy Department, 150, 152, 153, 158
Energy Research and Development Administration, 38, 150
Engler, Robert, 172
Environmental Protection Agency, 34, 38, 49, 58, 79, 91, 156
Environmental Sciences, Office of, 12
Equal Employment Opportunity Commission, 111-112
Eulau, Heinz, 172, 176
Executive Office of the President, 149-150

Farmers Home Administration, 25
Federal Aviation Administration, 114
Federal Bureau of Investigation, 62
Federal Energy Administration, 38, 150
Federal Energy Regulatory Commission, 150

Federal Judicial Center, 11
Federal Power Commission, 150
Federal Regional Councils, 78
Federal Register, 124, 125, 131
Federal Trade Commission, 129
Fenno, Richard F., 172, 174
Ferguson, Leroy, 172, 176
Food and Drug Administration, 156
Food and Nutrition Service, 155
Ford, Gerald R., 20, 45, 49, 67, 131, 133, 134, 137, 138, 143, 144, 145, 160, 161
Foreign Agricultural Service, 15

Gallup, George, 144, 175
Gellhorn, Ernest, 175
General Accounting Office, 68-69 84-85, 114
Gist, John R., 174
Goldwater, Barry, 54, 61
Governor's Conference, 62
Grants, 79-80, 81, 82, 83, 84, 86, 106, 113, 129
Griffith, Ernest, 60, 173
Grodzins, Morton, 79, 173
Gruenstein, Peter, 176
Gulick, Luther, 135

Hadwiger, Don F., 172
Halberstam, David, 46, 172
Hardin, Charles M., 172
Havemann, Joel, 176
Health Care Financing Administration, 151
Health, Education and Welfare, Department of (now the Department of Health and Human Services and the Department of Education), 13, 74, 75, 79, 115, 134, 151, 152
Health Insurance, Bureau of, 13
Health Manpower Education, Bureau of, 74
Hearings and Appeals, Office of, 130
Henry, Nicholas, 175
Higher Education, Bureau of, 16
Hoos, Ida R., 173
Hoover Commissions, 134, 135, 136, 138
Hoover, J. Edgar, 62, 63
Housing and Urban Development, Department of, 48-49, 75, 124, 151, 152, 167
Human Development, Office of, 151
Hunger lobby, 155

Incremental decisions, 108-109, 118

Independent Regulatory Commissions, 114, 120, 129, 130, 137-138, 150
Information Agency, U.S., 152
Interest groups, 26, 39, 54, 55-57, 59-60, 62, 63-64, 65, 82, 101, 114, 126, 144, 145, 154-155, 156, 158, 162, 163, 167
Intergovernmental relations, 78-81, 114, 161
Interior, Department of, 27-29, 40, 57-59, 70, 130
Internal Revenue Service, 98
International Communication, Agency for, 152
International Police Chiefs' Association, 62
Interpretive rules, defined, 125

Jewell, Malcolm E., 171
Johnson, Lyndon B., 45, 46, 47, 61, 62, 82, 135
Judges, bureaucratic, 127, 139
Judicial review of bureaucracy, 128-129, 136, 162
Justice, Department of, 13, 14, 61, 62, 82

Katzenbach, Nicholas, 61, 62, 63, 173
Kennedy, Edward, 108, 110
Kennedy, John F., 46, 94
Kennelly, Martin, 114
Kissinger, Henry, 45, 46, 145
Korea, 76
Kotz, Nick, 172, 173

Labor, Department of, 74, 76
Labor Statistics, Bureau of, 75
Lance, Bert, 148
Lardner, George, 176
Law Enforcement and Administration of Justice, Commission on, 61-62, 173
Law Enforcement Assistance Administration, 18, 61-63, 70, 71, 80, 81-85, 90, 91, 92, 93, 106, 116-117, 129, 153-154, 173
Legislative specialization, 50-54, 59-60, 63-64, 136-137, 161
Legitimacy of bureaucrats, 90, 92, 97, 99-101, 126, 161, 162, 163
Lewis, Eugene, 176
Libraries and Learning Resources, Bureau of, 13
Lindblom, Charles, 174
Lipsky, Michael, 176
Little city halls, 76

Little Hoover Commissions, 135
Lowe, Jeanne, 174

Management and Budget, Office of (formerly Bureau of the Budget), 23, 46, 68, 69, 75, 116, 135, 147-148, 151, 152
Manpower Administration, 14
Mansfield, Mike, 20
Marine Corps, 108, 109, 112-113
Martin, Edwin, 112-113
Matthews, David, 134
Matthews, Douglas, 172
Mayhew, David R., 173
McClellan, John, 62, 90
McNamara, Robert, 46
Meyerson, Martin, 174
Milbrath, Lester, 172
Minerals Policy Development, Office of, 27
Mines, Bureau of, 26-41, 70, 74, 76, 145
Mining Enforcement and Safety Administration, 27, 34, 35, 37, 74, 129-130, 172
Missions, defined, 12
Moe, Ronald D., 176
Murray, David, 174

National Association of Housing and Redevelopment Officials, 55
National Association of Manufacturers, 25, 56
National Coal Association, 39
National Education Association, 145, 175
National Highway Traffic Safety Administration, 104
National Institutes of Health, 95
National League of Cities, 39, 173, 174
National Nutrition Survey, 95
National Park Service, 25, 56
National Security Council, 66, 69
National Resources, Michigan Department of, 77, 97-98, 99-100, 122-123, 124, 129
New Federalism, 83, 84
Nonet, Philippe, 175
Nixon, Richard M., 12, 45, 47, 67, 83, 84, 136, 137

Paarlberg, Don, 154, 156, 176
Panama, 147
Patterson, Samuel C., 171
Pechman, Joseph, 174
Peirce, Neil, 176

Petroleum Association of America, 39
Piven, Frances Fox, 174
Planning and Programming, State Offices of, 67, 69
Planning, Programming, Budget System (PPBS), 68, 135, 175
Plotkin, Henry A., 175
Policy, defined, 15
Pomper, Gerald, 175, 176
Port of Oakland, 113
Pound, Roscoe, 175
Pressman, Jeffrey, 113, 174
Procedural rules, defined, 125
Program, defined, 12
Program development, defined, 17-19
Program evaluation, defined, 17-19
Program implementation, defined, 17-19
Progressive Movement, 9
Projects, defined, 107

Quade, E. S., 176

Reagan, Ronald, 134, 138
Reciprocity in Congress, 53, 59
Reclamation, Bureau of, 70
Red tape, 8, 163
Redburn, Thomas, 176
Regions, administrative, 78, 80, 81, 83-84, 93
Regulation, defined, 17-18
Reorganization, 137, 146-153, 158, 159-160
Reorganization Project, 147-148, 153, 160
Research capabilities of bureaucracy, 92, 96, 105-106, 110, 118-119, 169
Research, pure and applied, 32-33
Revenue sharing, 80, 82
Ribicoff, Abraham, 153
Ringquist, Delbert J., 172
Ripley, Randall B., 173
Rivlin, Alice, 171, 174
Robinson, Glen O., 175
Roethlisberger, F. J., 174
Rooney, John, 62
Roosevelt, Franklin D., 135

Schick, Allen, 173
Schuman, David, 171
Science and Technology, Office of, 67
Scientific management, 9
Scott, W. Richard, 173
Securities and Exchange Commission, 130
Sharkansky, Ira, 176
Sierra Club, 58
Simon, Herbert, 172, 173

Smithburg, Donald L., 173
Social Security Administration, 13, 151
Soviet Union, 15, 46, 147
Special Forces, U.S. Army, 93-94
Staffing, legislative and executive, 54, 58-59, 116, 147, 149-150, 162, 166-167
Stanton, Esther, 176
State, Department of, 46, 112-113, 145, 156
Stennis, John, 90
Stever, H. Guyford, 67
Strategic Air Command, 104-105, 107, 111
Student Financial Assistance, Bureau of, 151
Subgovernments (also whirlpools of activity), 60, 63-64, 65, 75, 101, 147, 148, 154, 163, 166
Substantive rules, defined, 125
Supreme Court, U.S., 122

Taylor, Frederick W., 9, 10, 171
Thompson, Victor, 173
Timpane, Michael, 174
Transportation, Department of, 155
Treasury, Department of, 49
Truman, David, 171
Truman, Harry S., 45
Tullock, Gordon, 173
Turkey, 46

Ujifusa, Grant, 172
United States Conference of Mayors, 173, 174
Urban Affairs, Local Departments of, 67, 69

Veteran's Administration, 76
Vietnam, 45, 46, 58, 93-94, 110, 111, 112-113
Wage and Price Stability, Council on, 138
Wahlke, John, 172, 176
Waldo, Dwight, 171, 174
Wallace, George C., 61, 134, 138, 143, 145-146
Watergate, 58
Watts, Harold, 174
Weber, Max, 7-9, 10-11, 13, 171
Weidenbaum, Murray, 173
Weiss, Carol, 175
West, Daniel, 176
White, Theodore H., 172, 176
Whitten, Jamie, 50, 53, 89
Wildavsky, Aaron, 113, 174
Witcover, Jules, 175